M.O.N.S.T.E.R. – PROOF
Your Child

Methods Of Nicely Silencing The Ego's Roar

Conscious Parenting Strategies

Lisa M. Smith, M.S., Msc.D., Ph.D.

Sealofters Press, Inc.

1061 East Indiantown Rd, Suite #104

Jupiter, FL 33477

Sealofters Press, Inc. was established in 2008 as a publishing alternative to the large, commercial publishing houses currently dominating the book publishing industry. Sealofters Press, Inc. is committed to publishing works of educational, cultural and community value.

Dedication

This book is dedicated to my most amazing teachers, my children: Stephanie, Kevin, Alexis, Kent and Riley. Without each of you, this book would not have been created. Stephanie, you taught me you are never too old to take a risk, reinvent yourself and dance blissfully! Kevin, you taught me about the process of accepting what "is" with grace and humor. Alexis, you taught me to stand in my own truth and never back down. Kent, you taught me about courage, hard work and determination and that even chores can be fun! Riley, you taught me to set boundaries, to embrace my inner goddess and the importance of fabulous shoes!

To my family: The one I was born into and the ones I have "added" along the way - thank you for your love and support!

"Life is either a daring adventure

or nothing at all."

Helen Keller

Table of Contents

Introduction

Parenting...it's not just an adventure... it's a job!
(And a rigorous one at that!)

There's nothing that can help you

understand your beliefs more

than trying to explain them

to an inquisitive child.

Frank A. Clark

It is 0-five hundred hours and you have checked in for your tour of duty. You have shown up fully prepared - with your new haircut, shiny new boots and pressed camouflage. You are in a dark room (where you will remain throughout your duty) and it is announced in a hushed tone (this is a sacred mission, after-all), that you are about to embark on the scariest, life-threatening, sanity-challenging, sleep-deprived, heralding mission of your life.

You will be pushed past your limits, you will need all of your resources (and even some you do not even possess yet), you will need to be able to speak many languages (from infant babble to teenage-hood – which by the way is a language that changes daily and as of yet, has still yet to be clearly defined), navigate through emotional choppy waters, repair wounded flesh and hearts, find innovative solutions to impossible problems at the drop of a hat, be in several places at once, have eyes in the back of your head, and not get your feelings hurt when you are shot at with intense words like "I hate you" and "you're the *worst*" countless times.

You will be in charge of a helpless being who will vomit on you, pee on you, kick you, possibly bite you and threaten your very sanity at times. You will never get a day off, a vacation, sick time, nor will you be paid for this. Lastly, there is NO manual. You will safely navigate this terrain with no map, no compass and you *will* be blindfolded.

However, you will gain skills like knowing where every bathroom is within a 10-mile radius of everywhere you go. You will have contents in your purse and/or vehicle that can feed a family of four for a week, maybe longer…a First Aid kit that rivals any decent EMT; will go to any length possible to get that ONE sought after Happy Meal toy and will be able to leap tall buildings in a single bound to remove a "choke-able" from your child's hand before ingestion. You will be able to identify each and every toy your child has just by stepping on it in the middle of the night.

You will learn to negotiate with grace and ease - from the two-year old who is holding the cat in one hand and an open bottle of vegetable oil in the other (over your new carpet) to the teenager wagging YOUR keys in front of YOU offering to go get groceries that YOU do not want nor need. You will learn an entirely new math system, where your money goes out and never comes back.

You will hear yourself say things that you swore would never come out of your mouth and find there are days when you do not even recognize the person staring back at you. You will most likely be referred to as "so-n-so's mother or father) – yes, you might lose your identify once in a while. You might even announce on occasion that you have to "go to the potty" (in the company of full-fledge adults, who most likely will not notice your vernacular). And it might only happen once, but most likely you will sound like your very own mother at some point during this adventure.

So, would you sign up for this tour of duty? Come on, who's in?

YOU – you know who you are…we just can't resist – we check the little box that says I know and understand (we have NO clue!), and sign on the dotted line - our former lives away. Yet, in spite of the disclosure - we all jump in blindfolded and all. Although all of the above are applicable, there are so *many* intangible, inexplicable and vast rewards that it makes it all worthwhile and we do it over and over again. Being a parent is the opportunity to allow this being who has come through you, not TO you, to learn from you but also to teach you. The journey I have taken with my children has forced me to examine my *own* fears and "Monsters" more closely. They are my Master teachers and as I have humbly sat at their feet, I learned so much about myself – my True Self.

We are never really prepared for parenthood, because it is a process. It becomes a buried treasure we uncover within our own selves. We read manuals, we take the advice from those who have been there, but ultimately it is a journey we take alone. This book is called "How To M.O.N.S.T.E.R.-Proof Your Child" – where monsters represent the ego. M.O.N.S.T.E.R. is an acronym for Methods Of Nicely Silencing The Ego's Roar. The ego purports that there is something to be afraid of, whether it is in the closet, under the bed or in our heads – it still *feels* very real. As we nurture the mind, body and spirit of our child, we do so for ourselves, as well. When we bring the monster out of the closet, we expose it in ourselves and this can be a daunting process. We can tell our child there is nothing to be afraid of, but that is not enough. We must show them that they have within their own being a Self, which is greater than anything outside of them. We do this in many ways.

The first way we do this is connecting to the Higher Self within our *own* being. We cannot give away what we do not possess. We cannot tell our child (at least not convincingly) that there is nothing to be afraid of when we ourselves have our own unquestioned fears. So, what's wrong with being afraid anyway? Well, I suppose nothing, if it serves a purpose (running from a Saber tooth

Tiger comes to mind). However, most of what we are generally afraid of has no basis in reality – they are just "monster" thoughts. So, it isn't really serving a purpose (except to keep us and our child up at night wondering, commiserating and well, just awake, which totally stinks!).

Being afraid and operating from *fear* is different. There are many times when we will have fears. It's o.k. It happens. What we hope to do is to parent in such a way that our children can *feel* the fears (and challenge the thoughts that create them) and move throughout their lives anyway. However, they do not base their decisions from a place of fear.

We do this by insulating them. This is accomplished by planting "seeds of awareness" in their growing minds, bodies and spirits. In a busy world and a hectic life, it has been my experience that the *little* moments are perfect windows of opportunity to do this: riding in the car, bath time, bedtime, making dinner. But, when we are aware of these principles, we parent on purpose. We take the opportunities as they arise to plant seeds.

Anyone can count the number of seeds in an apple,

but no one knows the number of apples in just one seed.

Anonymous

Having worked in the field of neurodevelopment, I have had the opportunity to learn a lot about how the brain works and how we as "humans" experience ourselves being human. In my observations I see that how the brain becomes whole is by integrating multiple systems. The eyes "team" together to see, which imprints a picture on the brain, which transfers that image to something the brain can relate to and we say, "Aha…it's an apple." When we hear a sound, we correlate it to something that is meaningful (either a voice that is comforting, or a sound that brings fear). An experience becomes more than just what we see, hear, touch or smell. It becomes all of that rolled into one - individual parts, yet one whole experience. A child that experiences sensory deprivation or sensory overload cannot accurately assimilate all of the things coming in and thus shuts down. This was the case with my son who was diagnosed with autism at age 3 ½. His inability to integrate all of these things left him curled in a ball on the floor rocking, trying to somehow keep the world from continually assaulting him. Slowly and methodically, we brought him back to our world by integrating him and the sensory pieces little by little.

It has been very similar with the other children I have worked with. The integration of life in little bitty pieces allows for the brain to assimilate it. The brain makes changes based on frequency, intensity, duration and consistency. So, a certain activity done for the right amount of time, the right intensity and for the correct number of times consistently will result in a change. If you think about it, it is how we live. We eat like this – not one big meal forever and that's it. We take in bit by bit, assimilate what we need and well, you know get rid of the rest. If we take in too much or too little, it is unhealthy. The dictionary defines integration as the process of making whole. To live in today's world and be a parent today requires a lot of integration. In order to do this we can start early and plant little seeds that grow as the child grows.

This is the intention of this book…a little at a time. I call this **Parenting On Purpose** using *Conscious Parenting Strategies*. These suggestions and activities help us create an "on purpose" mindfulness about how we engage in activities with our child and what we provide for them to facilitate their growth and learning. My hope is that these ideas spur some of your own that are individualized for you and your child. Happy Planting!

Lisa

To bring up a child in the way he should go, travel that way yourself once in a while.

Josh Billings

I Wonder

I gaze into the perfect house,
with the perfect décor
And I wonder….
What would my life be like
without stains on the carpet
Without handprints on the walls
Without mis-matched furniture because I chose
To buy a swing set instead of new furniture.
I wonder how it would feel to sit in a room with
No visible signs of a life because it is immaculate -
A picture in a magazine.
I wonder at night, when I would sit alone
On the couch – how would that feel?
Sometimes, I think it might feel grand –
Like I am a Queen in a castle with perfectly
Arranged furniture and flowers just right
Arranged on a table.
I see the floor and it shines.
I see the pantry and everything is
Perfectly lined up.
I wonder…
Then, I settle back into my worn out couch
And I see pink and purple streaks on the floor
Remnants from a one-of-a-kind art project that
Was created mere moments ago.
I see a shoe that was cast off in a rush

To put on clickety-clack shoes –
After all, the Ball waits for no Princess.
And is that lipstick on the carpet?
Hot pink is my guess…it's the only color
The Princess wears.
And a handprint on the wall from the
Master Chef who made mud pies outside for
A spectacular feast and forgot to wash off her hands
Before pressing against the wall.
She must serve them fresh and hot, of course.
And little wood chips scattered around.
As our little hamster adds his own fragments of color
to the canvas
I call my life.
I wonder…
How could my life ever get any fuller -
Any richer in color than at this VERY moment?
There will never be a day like this, when
I entertained a Princess,
Ate the most magical
Mud pies
and saw a Masterpiece in the making.
I wonder,
At the perfection
In it all.

Lisa Smith
Mother of 5
2012

Play

Always jump in the puddles!

Always skip alongside the flowers.

The only fights worth fighting

are the pillow and food varieties.

Terri Guillemet

Lisa Smith, M.S., Msc.D., Ph.D.

There are some things you

learn best in calm,

and some in storm.

Willa Cather

Chapter 1 - Play

The M.A.G.I.C. Of Play!

There is a place where the formlessness of spirit meets the human form. It is a place of wonderment and magic. A place to meet your True Self and know it is You.

It is where you drop into all that you already are and if only for a moment forget everything you *think* you know about who you are....where the possibilities are endless. You cannot reach this place through your mind, although it is invited to tag along. Nor is it merely a physical experience, although the body joins with its energy and rhythms.
It is a place that is still, but not quiet.
It is empty, but not devoid.
It is powerful but not out of control.

It is the sacred space of play.
Where all of the lines on the page magically disappear leaving nothingness from which all is possible.
It is a safe space we can connect to our Higher Selves - our own inner giggle.

Love is a better teacher than duty.

Albert Einstein

The M.A.G.I.C. Of Play!

Kids: they dance before they learn

there is anything that isn't music.

~William Stafford

The American Academy of Pediatrics published a study highlighting the importance of play. They state that play is essential to development because it contributes to the cognitive, physical, social and emotional well-being of children. It is so important, as a matter of fact, that it has been recognized by the United Nations High Commission for Human Rights as a RIGHT for every child![1] Wow! That is incredibly powerful.

Yet, how many children "play" today? Statistics from 5 years ago (so imagine how they have changed since then), show that over the past two decades, the hours children have for "unstructured play" and outdoor activities have decreased by eight hours a week and overall free time by a total of twelve hours a week. The number of hours children spend in an organized sport has doubled and the time spent in "passive spectator leisure" (as in not moving!) has increased from thirty minutes to over three hours![2] Most children are hurried from one endless stream of activities to more endless streams of activities. We call them "enrichment" programs. But, one has to ask oneself…who is actually getting "rich" from these activities? The staggering statistics

5

show us that free play has dropped dramatically. The days of sitting around making something out of nothing have all but deteriorated. Parents have a lot of pressure to make sure that heir child is ready to meet the demands of the world, including preparation for college that begins in elementary school! Many working families have to rely on daycare and there are fewer families that have adult supervision during the workday. We have become incredibly efficient and tend to have task-oriented activities in all that we do, including play. We have turned parenting into a JOB that is complete with "to-dos", flow charts, quarterly statements and "Am I getting my money's worth?" mindsets. To get into college, kids are doing some pretty crazy things (some students are "cheating", tripling their majors or taking multiple athletic and artistic activities to "beef up" their résumés).

This hurried lifestyle has created stress and anxiety that can lead to depression. A survey by the American College Health Association showed that 61% of college students are feeling hopeless. Probably about how you're feeling right now after reading all of this, huh? I really do not like this kind of information. In general, I find it negative and unhelpful. But, it *is* necessary to understand why play is so important if we're going to make it a priority (which means de-prioritizing a lot of other things in our lives). We all have to look at the statistics and facts, if only for a moment so that we understand what we are up against and that it is an issue that we cannot ignore. We all know of the crisis within our country right now surrounding the topic of bullying. Kids are walking around half-full or some of them, plain empty. But, there is hope (ah…I promise). There is something we can do and it is not going to mean selling all of your worldly possessions and moving out into the forest in a lean-to.

What is the answer? What can we do about this?

The Weber Fechner law is a principle that states that the level of what it is that you can detect or perceive is dependent on the background noise or distraction. The more background noise, the more signal you need.

Or you need to lower the background noise.

We live in a world with a lot of background noise. It is difficult to hear our children's signals, let alone read them. In order to do that, we need to lower the noise. We do this by dropping into a sacred space with our child. We play. Play has been proven to be an incredible way to help children build confidence, master their environment and most importantly, foster a connection with their parents and family, which is essential for creating resilience. This is one incredibly important, efficient, and fun way we "monster-proof" our kids. The study conducted by the American Academy of Pediatrics states that kids who are likely to gain the essential traits of resiliency are those children who come from a home where there is unconditional love and a connection…time together. [3]

Play facilitates this!

So, what is play anyway? What does it do? Does it serve a purpose at all or is it just something kids do until they "grow up" and learn about the real world? Have you ever watched a child immersed in play? They are not having a playful experience. They ARE the playful experience. It's like they step into a little portal that takes them into an entirely other world.

I love the Movie *Hook* with Robin Williams and Dustin Hoffman. Peter is all grown up and a high-power executive. He goes back to visit Wendy, who is now elderly. His children are kidnapped by Hook and Peter has to retrieve them. However, he has forgotten his Essence. He does not remember how to play. But his "shadow" – self reminds him of his ability to play, while Tinkerbelle shouts the mantra "Believe" and to think of happy thoughts, which make you fly. Peter reclaims his ability to play, thus saving his children (and his family in the process and he "connects" to his son, with whom he has lost touch with – which is the BEST part of the movie!) His reconnection to his inner Essence, which he finds through play saves his family, oh and him too!

One thing I consistently have talked about with my own children is that we cannot give away what we do not have. We cannot give love, hope, joy, peace, contentment, laughter…etc., if we ourselves are not experiencing them. One issue that we all tend to "grow out of" is our ability to play with life. We become like Peter, with our oh-so-busy-and-consuming lives and forget to play with, through and in our lives.

8

We start out so incredibly intuitive about this. If you don't believe me, go spend the day with a bunch of 2-5 year olds. They totally rock! In their world, ANYTHING (and everything) is possible and most likely probable. They create out of nothing, move effortlessly from flying in a rocket ship to making scrumptious delights out of mud to rescuing kittens as a fire fighter to making forts with blankets and tents where they attend worlds not yet imagined and they do it over and over again, each experience as joyous and new as the one before.

When is the last time you let your "inner play" out?

Another great movie I enjoyed while doing research is *Mr. Magorium's Wonder Emporium,* where play is the order of the day…where the magic and wonder is not just reserved for those who "can't see over the counter yet." Now, a lot of people will say, "Well, I golf – that's play" (or something of the sort). That may or may not be true, but generally, for most people when you do anything that "keeps score" it stops being play. It happens. There are different types of play. Authentic play has no rules, does not keep score and allows you to wiggle around boundless!

Do you know that statistically a child's self-esteem is the highest in pre-school and declines when they start school? This ironically starts the process of "keeping score." Now, I'm not impugning team sports or recreational activities such as golf. They're great and have their place in the world. But real play does not keep score.

We have to stop and take a look and see exactly what is it that our child is learning about play, competition and "winning." When my daughter was 5, she tried out playing soccer (and when I mean tried out, I mean it didn't fit – but, we made it through the season by playing in the dirt in the goalie box!) After our first game, the coach told them the "score" and she asked me what it meant. I told her it was the number of times each team kicked the ball into the goal. Another child heard me and chimed in, "Yea, and the team with the most points at the end wins – we won!" The kids erupted in cheer and Riley says, "Oh, I thought we were just having fun." Yea, me too-kid. Welcome to the world of keeping score! They learn so early that there is a winner and a loser and in order to survive, well, you know what side you need to be on. Research tells us that when winning is the goal, learning is not happening. It would probably be a whole other book to discuss this topic in full, but suffice it to say our children learn about play from us. It becomes a conundrum to discuss the concept of "unity" and "we are all one" when clearly our society would indicate that we do "take sides" and compete.

Real play or "original play" has an integral place in our lives and in our children's lives. Focusing on what we want to expand in our children becomes the focus of our definition of play. There are many definitions for the word play. I prefer this one: *Play refers to a range of voluntary, intrinsically, motivated activities that are normally associated with pleasure and enjoyment* (if you're not giggling, at least inside, it's probably not play!)

10

One quality of play is that it involves movement - because energy moves…how many hours in the day are we not moving (driving, sitting at a desk, sitting down in front of the TV)? Think about it. And I don't mean movement for the purpose of going from A to B – or running on a treadmill to get your exercise. Genuine Play is not movement so much for the sake of getting somewhere but of *being* somewhere…being fully present with your inner giggle. Yes, I just made that up. But, it expresses exactly what play is. I read this delicious quote that said, "Laughter is a smile that bursts!" I love it! An inner giggle is laughter that embodies your entire being.

So, before we can understand it outside of ourselves as in recognize and nurture it within our children we have to see what it is inside of us. If you're not sure, check out the movie *BIG* with Tom Hanks, or *Mr. Magorium's Wonder Emporium* or *Charlie and the Chocolate Factory* or just go jump on a trampoline or swing at the park – find the part of you, (if you have lost touch with it) that still giggles at bathroom noise (come on, they're funny) and finds wonder sitting under a home-made tent in the living room or that can still make something out of nothing.

Or just do the hokey pokey! Yes, you heard me…put your right hand in and shake it all about!

What if the hokey-pokey is what it's all about?

Think of the magic in this song. You put your "right" hand in – which, according to energy medicine is the side of your body that "actualizes" what it is you wish to create in the world, the "left" hand in (which is the side of your body that receives) and you put your head in (filled with thoughts, beliefs and ideas that you have assimilated over a lifetime which according to research may or may not even be true!) and then your whole self in and "shake it all about" which is to say – you question it – you shake things up a bit…then you turn yourself around (go in an entirely new direction) and what do you say??

Hokey Pokey – which is like "Hocus Pocus!" Which is he word used for Magic…**M.A.G.I.C.** (And I love to make acronyms – they help me to remember concepts – so, here's one -- **M**ANIFESTING **A**WARENESS (**M.A.**) **I**NNER **C**ONNECTEDNESS (**I.C.**) WITH **G**OD RIGHT THERE IN THE MIDDLE!) that's what I'm talking about! Let's make some magic…in ourselves and in our children! For play IS magic….it's Alice in Wonderland meets Buddha! Peacefully surrendering, letting go and dropping into the magical proverbial hole (whole?) of bliss where *anything* is possible.

Once we connect to that Inner Essence within ourselves, we can connect with the Essence in our children. If you're not sure, just begin…you cannot get wet from the "word" water – you just have to jump in and guess what? I bet your kids will be more than happy to teach you how to play…really play! Just ask them!

Now, we're ready to play!

"Unlikely adventures require unlikely tools."

(Mr. Magorium in Mr. Magorium's Wonder Emporium)

Dr. Stuart Brown is the founder of the National Institute For Play and has studied the qualities and effects of play for over twenty years. It is not just an important biological process but it has an incredible impact on the brain and its development. He has studied the animal kingdom and even animals on the lower end of the food chain play. He has discovered that the animals that play more have the best survival rate. Why? Play serves a purpose by allowing animals to pretend and practice the skills that are necessary for survival. In play, animals get to "try out" their skills in a non-threatening way. A study was conducted and those species who played less had smaller brains (this was all relative to size). But not only do they learn how to hone their skills, they learn how to harness and regulate them as well.[4] Why spend more energy than necessary?

What is so great is that kids know this innately. When my son was diagnosed with autism, this system short-circuited and my son no longer played. He manipulated things, but the essence, the joy behind the wonderment of play had vanished. In its place was a boy who didn't seem capable of enjoying life. As he was able to assimilate life back into his world a little at a time, the joy returned. He is at 21 one of the most playful young men I have known (although you would not know it from his quiet and serious demeanor). But, I love watching

13

him do chores – everything is a game. He has found the secret to life. Being happy is a state of being. A state you find in play.

Original Play

God sleeps in the stories,

Dreams in the plants,

Stirs in the animals,

Awakens in humanity

And plays in us all.
Anonymous

There are studies out of the University of Washington that indicate that parents spending **15 minutes a day** in this **state of play with their child** have **substantially decreased a wide range of behavioral problems**. It's not just about teaching our children how to play. It is about embracing the essence of ourselves that is free of judgment and attachment. Then we can connect *that* part of ourselves to the part of our child that already and inherently knows this. Fred Donaldson has been watching and learning from children for years. In his book, *Playing By Heart: The Vision and Practice of Belonging*, he discusses his twenty plus years of research in this area. He says that when we play we are actually creating the possibility of a new "we" out of "you" and "I."[5] Our connection with something greater than ourselves starts in this moment. When we are able to connect on this profoundly deep level, I'm pretty sure that there is nothing else that will come up during childhood that cannot be handled.

I tried to teach my child with books,

He gave me only puzzled looks.

I tried to teach my child with words,

They passed him by, often unheard.

Despairingly, I turned aside,

"How shall I teach this child?" I cried.

"Come," he said, "Play with me."

Anonymous

The beauty of play is that there really is no objective...you don't have to have any rules and certainly do not need to accomplish anything. As a matter of fact, if you do – it is most likely *not* play. Striving for play is like screaming for silence – it's an oxymoron. Play is a coming together in this space where there is emptiness but not nothingness. Play gently manifests from the stillness. Like the silence between the notes that creates music, the stillness or emptiness provides the space for something to come forth. Here we create something BECAUSE of the lack of something else. And that something else or lots of "somethings" – are rules, expectations, thoughts about what we should or should not do, preconceived notions and pretty much all of the baggage we haul around each and every day. Here, in this place it is all dropped – suspended in a moment of pure essence and P.L.A.Y. (perpetually laughing at your "self" (the smallest part of you that IS the baggage).

If you haven't time to respond to a

tug at your pants leg,

your schedule is too crowded.

Robert Brault

I have formulated what I call the **Qualities of Play**, which are like Rules, except they're not…. they're more like guidelines – because there really are no rules in play (can I emphasize this enough? ☺).

- There is a sense of wonderment coupled with a lack of fear.
- What "we know" is set aside.
- There are no limits – time, space – the possibilities are endless.
- It perpetuates joy & laughter so much that you might actually lose yourself.
- It creates a sense of oneness.

Play – it is not something you do – it is something that you become. Donaldson says, "Like the wood of Gepetto, our bodies, minds and hearts are touched in play until all that is unnecessary is removed. This is practicing; it is how we become playmates."[6]

Observe your child in play. Look at their eyes and their very beings as they drop all that they know about reality

and become completely immersed in the new reality they are creating. I imagine if we were able to connect them and look at their brains during this time, all of the neurons firing and wiring together would rival any good Fourth of July show. Children embody, act out and bring to life stories. They *are* the storytellers. Play is the place where we can sit at the feet of (or if we're really lucky, wrestle around with) these storytellers and learn.

Play allows a child to communicate and process. They innately understand that there is an inner being, a higher Self that witnesses all that goes on. This is something that takes most of us our entire adult life to "re-member". When children play, they *become* the witness and "play out" their life dramas as though they were playing a part. How smart is that? If we could all play with our life dramas that way, the world would be, well, more playful and most likely more peaceful.

When my daughter was eight, her and her brother had a playful ritual they would engage in each night. Kent is endlessly patient with Riley, who can be quite demanding at times. Sometimes, this playtime lead to tears, for no apparent reason. Well, at least not apparent to me. But, yet, it seems like a "playful dance" both necessary and therapeutic, so I did not intervene. One night, after a playful time that ended in tears, I was holding Riley and she told me why she cried. She said, "Sometimes, at school when so-and-so says mean things to me, I cannot cry. I really want to, but she will call me a crybaby. So, at night all of those cries want to come out and this lets me get them out." Wow! I was amazed at her insight and her "knowingness" that this play served a very important purpose for her.

If I had intervened (because, it seemed like she was not enjoying it, as it ended in tears), I would have robbed her of some very good self-induced therapy! Sometimes "bad" feelings come up during play. It's o.k. We need to let it flow because it is incredibly therapeutic for getting all of the stressors of the day (and our kids are inundated with them today!) out. Once she became aware of this, we worked with other ways for her to cope with this situation at the time it happens. But if it were not for the safe space of play, she would not have discovered it in the first place.

Think about yourself when you have a bad day or stressful day. I'll bet you have some coping mechanism in place, if only to soak in a tub, conversation with a spouse or a good friend, or going for a walk. But, children do not have access to coping mechanisms, so we need to teach them ways to cope with these things that happen during the day and the feelings that come up. Play provides a natural forum for the excavation of thoughts and feelings. Having those feelings all tangled up inside can make a child very, very sad (depression) or very, very angry (aggressive/bully). Feelings need to be processed. Play is the perfect foreground for that.

So, what does play have to do with eliminating fear (as in "monster-proofing" your child)? Fear, the opposite of love, acts as a gateway by which doubt for what we really know in Essence comes through. It comes through by way of thoughts. All of these thoughts are based on a lack of connectedness. When *we* connect to something greater than ourselves (which we do inherently in play) and pass that connection on by way of example or during play to our children we create a different foundation of thought that is based in truth. Research shows that children learn through imitation and they actually adopt our beliefs up until about age 6 or 7. Neuroscience shows that kids from ages 2-6 spend most of their time in theta brain wave frequencies. This is the brain wave frequency that hypnotherapists try to evoke when utilizing hypnosis.[7] In other words, our kids are assimilating a lot of information subconsciously at this time! We want to playfully and "on purpose" foster beliefs of resiliency, which will "monster-proof" them for life! When we convey a sense of connectedness to a higher source, our children feel that and can imitate that. This connection begins with us and play fosters and nurtures that connection. We get to play around with ideas, thoughts and even imaginary parts of ourselves. Kids get to test out how strong they are and different aspects of themselves. The creativity and bursting imagination that play facilitates is unparalleled.

I watch how children do this everyday. They play store or restaurant and if there are no cups available, something else becomes the cup. They are unattached to "form" – things do not have to come in a certain package to work. In the world of play, anything and everything is possible. Stuffed animals come to life, become dressed up and join tea parties as if they are royalty. You can put on a costume and transform yourself into someone completely different. You can fly, leap across rainbows, and experience a life filled with wonder, joy and bliss and completely free of fear. When you play you *become* the experience – you are one with it.

An amazing and wonderful healing tool used with children is play therapy. It allows them to play-out their fears and concerns and even traumas that have happened to them. When my daughter was experiencing a bully issue at school, we used play to solve it. She was safe to act out her feelings in play, which allowed her to transfer it into reality. I'm pretty sure that is a formula for success right there!

So, how do you play, *really* play with your child? The best way I know how it to connect to a part of yourself and something you really enjoy and share that experience with your child. I do not particularly like to play Barbies. I never have. I used to force myself to do it. However, this was not lost on my older daughter. So, one day, I decided maybe I could play something else. What!? Seriously, it does not have to be drudgery? Yes, that's the point – if you are not having fun, most likely, neither is your child.

20

So, I found things I enjoyed doing and we made those our wonderful play moments. I would still play Barbies on occasion and would try to find ways in which I could play authentically (my Barbies usually sang or did wild, feminist-like things!) but, the point is, we played it out. One moment we have enjoyed together is taking baths together and drawing on each other's backs and making "silly" drinks in the bathtub, getting out and setting up a tea party on my bed and coloring together. I love baths and I love coloring! Sharing this experience together has become an amazing experience for both of us. I love to sing, so we put music on in our house and dance around the house singing. While making dinner, I have been known to pick up a cucumber and dance around the kitchen to delightful squeals and giggles. It's fun! Almost each night, we have a nightly wrestling ritual. It only lasts 5 minutes (I don't have *that* much energy by nighttime!), but it is enough to allow us to connect, playfully and for my daughter to feel strong and resilient when she pins me to the bed!

Dr. Lawrence Cohen in *Playful Parenting* (a book I highly recommend!) talks about kids as having cups and they need to continually have their cups replenished.[8] This is accomplished through play. Kids want so much to connect with us that this allows us all to drop our guards (I mean, seriously, Mom is so much more approachable when you have seen her singing love songs to a cucumber!) and allow ourselves to play with life and our children. The beautiful thing about nurturing this within ourselves and our homes is that it provides a "safe space" forever. What I mean by that is, as your children grow, you have all of these strung-together moments of shared laughter and joy. It bonds you so that when things get sticky, there is something to fall back on. When the "not-so-warm-and-fuzzy" feelings come up, you have a forum to release them and process them. You have created a friendly, "cease-fire" zone where all who enter feel safe and free to be themselves and are unconditionally loved and accepted there. Wow! That's a place anyone would want to be, don't you think?

Dr. Cohen says, "It takes a village idiot to raise a child!" [9] It is probably one of my favorite things he says in his great book. What he means by this is, don't be afraid to play the fool, be a goof-ball. I mean think of *you* from your child's perspective. You've got it all going on. You have the money, the keys to the car, the right to buy (or not buy) any food, clothes, or toys YOU want. You pick out everything, make the rules and on and on. The power is definitely in our favor as parents. Not only that, adding insult to injury – we tend to know a whole lot more than our kids, just by nature of having lived through our mis-haps already. Of course, if you ask a teenager, we're dumb as dirt – but, you know what I mean! The point of this for me, join them…where they are in a place of play. Wherever that is, on the floor, wrestling matches, bubble baths, Barbies (yikes!), their music, their movies, their coffee drinks…it's magical and the illusion of being separate melts away!

"No matter what they tell you,

you don't have to color inside the lines."

(Mr. Magorium in Mr. Magorium's magic emporium)

Play and the Brain

My daughter, at 5 years old asked me for a DS. The request was followed by the question, "What's a DS?" (Note to self, if she doesn't know quite what it is, she's probably not ready for it.) So, I asked her why she wanted one. Well, because so-and-so has one, of course. "Hmm…" I pondered. "I'll think about that one when your birthday comes up, but part of me is saying it is not a good idea right now." And I left it at that. About 10 minutes later, she came out of her room. She had ripped the pages out of an old diary that was approximately DS size and made her own. It had stickers, and she had written all kinds of things on it. She had created in fantasy what she could not have in reality! And oh, the neuron connections she had made – woohoo! She also had made an iPod. I was talking to her and she said, "Hold on, I need to pause my music." She hit the "pause" button on this little iPod she had made, talked to me, hit the pause button again and preceded to "sing" the song that was playing! The neurodevelopmental specialist in me was jumping up and down! I could almost see the connections being made right in front of my eyes! You cannot buy this kind of brain development at the toy store!

Now, it would have been easy to get her DS – and I'm not saying that at some point I won't. My son has a PSP that he got at age 15. We do not have any other gaming stations at our house (his father has a Wii, which is totally awesome!) and I am not against technology but to some degree it can inhibit creative play. However, in moderation, these things can be a nice treat to augment the oh-so-hearty "Meal" of play. Kind of like how sweets and deserts are to eating. Eaten sparingly and with great gusto, they can be super, duper fun! However, when they become the "main course," we're headed for trouble and serious deficiencies.

One important part of play is the propensity for endless possibilities. However, if it has already been created, what's the point? For example, toys that come with just one thing to do (usually those with an on/off switch) are highly unimaginative. However, give a kid a box of blocks, dress-up stuff, crayons, glue, a miscellaneous assortments of art supplies, blank canvases, old boxes (you are probably getting the picture), and we have masterpieces just waiting to happen (and a whole lot of neuron firings taking place!) I am not against toys. At our house, we have a bunch and are continually getting more. We have a rule, though – when we get something new, we give something away. We are constantly recycling things in the garage to "take turns" with new things. But, when we are planting seeds of awareness, we want to have a child who can think outside the box (inside and all around it too!).

We cannot talk about play without talking about video games, technology and the Internet. Not that these things are bad but recent research has shown us that the plasticity of our brains (the ability to make changes), lasts up until about the time we die. We literally have the ability to change our brains. This is good news AND bad news…given the "wrong conditions" by which they can be changed. Currently there are no long-term studies that show the affects technology has on the brain. We are in a serious gray area and we just need to be conscious of that.

Now, granted, I get why we give our kids things to keep them quiet…trust me. I have a child that came out of the womb talking. While working in the field of neuroscience, we brought my daughter in to do a brainmap. While doing this, we do a Cognitive Ability's test (like an IQ test). After completing the test, my colleague said to me, "she's linguistically gifted" – really!? Is that what you're calling it – please, sometimes I think my head just might explode – she even talks in her sleep! Now, granted, in her defense, she gets it naturally. Her mother and father are talkers. My dad would laugh when he would recall the story of me talking incessantly to this little girl I met while we were camping at age 6. Her parents came over to thank my parents because the little girl didn't have a lot of friends and also, to let them know that she was deaf! That did not stop me!

So, I understand why we do it, sometimes. We just have to have a clear understanding of what it is doing to our child's growing and developing self so that we don't "over do" it. We are traversing into gray areas of technology. There are so many wonderful benefits to online access, yet children have access to information that they might not be ready for.

Here are a few facts from the media clearing house and the Nielson's 2012 Social Media Report[10]. Over half of teenagers 12 and over have a profile page. 72% of middle school students spend over 3 hours per day in front of a computer, on a phone or in front of a TV. Compared to 2004 when less than half of teenagers owned a cell phone, in 2008 the percentage went up to 72% (ages 12-17). An article in the Chronicle showed that 51% of teenagers check the status of their profile page more than once a day and 39% have posted something they regret later. 18% of children under the age of 7 go online. Kids as young as age 2 can use a mouse! There are critics who are concerned that early access to computers can greatly interfere with a child's ability to interact socially and can "change the brain" – but not in a good way.

Games on the Internet encourage short-attention spans by using sounds and lights to capture attention and provide instant gratification. Children who spend a great deal of time playing the computer can and are literally changing their brains. In addition, kids are getting a cyberspace social network, which may not be in their best interest. Also, children growing and developing should be physically active. Some experts suggest that children under the age of 7 not even be on the computer at all.[11]

When our children spend a lot of time sitting, either playing a computer game, or video game or anything that keeps them sedentary, the energy that they are building up (and you know they are by the mouth noises they make when they don't get to the next level on the game they're playing), builds up inside their bodies. They have no outlet for that. What we do know is that when children are engaged in video games, watch their eyes glaze over and they manifest stress-like symptoms in their bodies. They are creating a lot of energy inside of their bodies and not letting it out because they are sitting still. In a study that was conducted, it was noted that as soon as the TV was turned on, kids consistently stopped playing.

Not to mention, they are spending a great deal of time *sitting* (as in not moving) during school, now and with many schools having eliminated P.E. and diminished recess time, our kids (especially more active and kinesthetic learners, have no outlet for all of this energy). Could there be a correlation between that and the onslaught of ADD/ADHD? While reading Dr. Brown's book, *Play* and after the first chapter it hit me – children have stopped playing and we have an increase in ADD/ADHD over the past twenty years. Wow! I sat in silence for a few moments absorbing this thought. Well, a few chapters later Dr. Brown makes the same assertion, so it was not an original thought, but it is an alarming one. Research shows us that play – *real* play affects the brain's frontal cortex and our ability to think. It also affects the cerebellum, which is responsible for rhythm and children with ADD/ADHD struggle with timing – like their pace-setter is not set appropriately. Play shapes the brain. Sitting still does not. It's just that simple.

It seems that times are changing more rapidly than we think. Having worked with many children with Asperger's syndrome, which manifests a lot as deficiencies in language and social interactions, I know what this "looks like" in children. I am increasingly disturbed at the number of typically developing kids today who do not interact socially (as in face-to-face) very much. Kids can be in the same car, texting to one another. Texting, Facebooking, Tweeting, Instagramming are all part of the new social "norm" – a forum by which kids ask each other out and even break up with one another. It's such an issue that on a popular television program, *Modern Family,* the family tried to go a week without technology and the parents had just as hard of time as the kids! I am not proposing an all or nothing scenario. I just want to create awareness around this topic. We need to be aware and conscious of the time our children (and ourselves?) spend using technology.

One problem with texting and "Facebooking" is the lack of personal contact. The issue is that it is devoid of emotion and does not require that the person making the statement observe or take into account, the reactions of the person receiving the information. This "face-to-face" (not "face-to-Facebook") interaction is incredibly important to the social development of a child, not to mention a conscience. Emotional Intelligence is something we want to foster in our children. We want them to be able to have empathy and understanding. This does not happen without human interaction. One area or skill that cannot be developed without human interaction is the ability to read facial

29

expressions, body language and non-verbal cues. If one says something that hurts the feelings of another, seeing that reaction is a lot more difficult to take in and then subsequently say more hurtful things. Children can become desensitized to the emotions of others without this "human" interaction. Remember only 7% of communication is the words we use, 93% of ALL communication is non-verbal. Our tone and body language comprise most of our communication.

Parents are still the single most important factor in play. We are still the "gatekeepers" of what is played, when it's played and how it is played. We set up opportunities and influence either directly or indirectly a child's perception about play and their ability to engage in play.

One way to investigate the quality of play your child is having is a "Play Journal" – how many hours during the week and weekend is your child playfully playing? Keep a journal for a week. How many hours is your child: watching TV, playing the computer, playing a video game, texting, listening to an iPod or anything with an on/off switch? How many hours do they use their large muscles in play? How often does your child "make something out of nothing?" How many hours of "free time" does your child get on a weekly basis to just sit, ponder and create? How many hours is your child engaged in a "structured" (as in rules made by someone else) activity versus "unstructured" activity? (See journal at the end of this chapter).

Based on the research of what a child needs, the following is a "play pyramid." It works like the old food pyramid we memorized as a child. What we want is more of the types of play on the bottom, and less of the play that is on the top. "Sweets" (in referencing the food pyramid) are not forbidden, they are just limited and we are selective about what, when and how much. It would serve us and our children well to think about play in a similar fashion.

Play is often talked about as if it were a relief from serious learning. But for children play is serious learning. Play is really the work of childhood.
Mr. Rogers

The Play Pyramid®

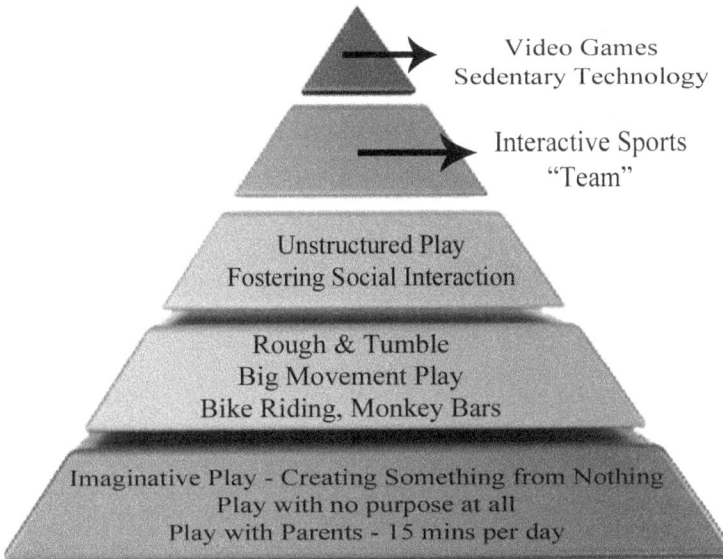

Video Games
Sedentary Technology

Interactive Sports
"Team"

Unstructured Play
Fostering Social Interaction

Rough & Tumble
Big Movement Play
Bike Riding, Monkey Bars

Imaginative Play - Creating Something from Nothing
Play with no purpose at all
Play with Parents - 15 mins per day

Playful Suggestions

"We don't stop playing because we grow old; we grow old because we stop playing."

George Bernard Shaw

Perspective Taking Game

This is a game I like to play beginning when a child first learns to talk. It is a game we teach but we learn so much in teaching it. With the concept of "planting seeds" – we want to invoke a sense of oneness within our child from the moment they are born. We do this by looking at (and pointing it out to our child) how we are all alike. We can talk of this when our child is an infant.

Then, when they talk, we can point it out to them. We can look at a magazine or a TV program, and ask the child, "How are you like that little girl?" (Ah…she says, "We both have blond hair, or pink shoes etc.). Then, you can go to the playground, or mall, or anywhere and do the same thing. What is great about this is when you begin to expand ("How am I like the rock, the cloud?"), it stretches the imagination, but it fosters a sense of connectedness with other things and other beings. When this "seed" grows, it will be all the child knows. They will see how they are "alike" and not so much how they are different. Can you just imagine a world where that is how we all saw each other? Wow.

Another "perspective taking" game is to look at trash on the ground. "Hmm…I wonder how the ground feels about that?" Or when your child sees another child in pain, "I wonder how that feels." Or a child being yelled at, "What do you think he is feeling right now?" Remember our kids are learning to imitate from the ages of 2-6. They

35

are watching and storing away into their sub-conscious the foundation of who they will be. Makes you want to make sure you are "planting on purpose" huh?

GOT PLAY?

What if, as an adult, with your "I'm the parent and have to be responsible" hat on, it's very hard for you to just loosen up and let go. Here are a few suggestions for YOU to get your play on (remember, we can't give away what we ourselves do not possess!):

- Get a joke book
- Download some silly songs
- Find a few ridiculous YouTube videos to watch or a silly movie
- Jump on a trampoline…it's really hard not to laugh when you do this!
- Suck a lollipop
- Get bubblegum – real bubblegum and blow bubbles
- Shoot a water gun
- Play Jax
- Jump rope
- Color
- Play with play dough
- Finger-paint (with pudding, and lick your fingers!)
- Play with matchbox cars
- Go to the park (alone) and swing.

Mostly…try to remember what you used to do that you *loved* more than anything…. Then, go do that!

Remember what it was like to be a kid?

Remember the magic in mud pies, forts,

playing dress-up

and making something out of nothing?

You may have left it behind.

But it's never forgotten you.

I hear it calling your name.

Playful suggestions

Pair something you or your child do not like (cleaning) with something you do like (fun music, chewing gum, etc.)

Make "Play breaks" when doing homework or anything challenging. Set a timer or give your child an indication of when it's coming. "After you do 5 math problems, you can ___ for 5 minutes."

Schedule play for you and your family weekly. Get a Got Play!? Jar that everyone can add suggestions to.

Playful Family Night suggestions

Camp-in (make a tent, have pizza and s'mores in an indoor tent).

"Lights out" night…where you use candles and pretend that you don't have any electricity – like you live in the stone ages. Give everyone jobs….and when it's time for lights on…make a big production as if you all have created light & electricity – beating on your chests and roaring (think Tom Hanks in the movie "Cast Away", when he created fire!)

Eat Dessert First night.

Once a month (or once a week) let someone be the "Star" – they get to pick out the food for dinner, showcase something (artwork, dance, or entertain the family).

Scavenger hunt – hide something small for everyone (could be a small candy bar for desert) and leave a "clue" on their plate.

Family wrestling match.

Flashlight tag.

Hide n seek.

Name that tune…play a game where you play a few bars of music and "contestants" have to hit a bell or buzzer and name the song.

Game night (Star of the week gets to choose the game the family plays).

Put on a song and dance – do the chicken – learn a new dance together (better yet, let your child teach you some new moves…always interesting).

"Movie night" at home – using monopoly money (or have kids make it, the more involved they are, the more they'll enjoy this), have popcorn, candy, etc. – that they can "buy"…my kids always loved this!

"Fancy Dinner at home night" (where you dress up, use the best dishes, wine glasses for the kids, make a toast….more than one fork (it's a great way to teach etiquette, but also have some fun doing it!) I actually hired a neighbor kid to come serve us – he loved it and the kids thought it was so cool!

Simon Says or Follow The Leader (especially good for a child struggling with "leading" or is getting picked on…gives them a sense of power to "direct the adults" in his or her life.

Make "human structures" create a "family" machine, where everyone has to participate and "add" something. Everyone (individually) writes their name for the structure on an index card and what the "machine" does. Then, share with each other.

Or "Bet you Can't Get Away" – playfully holding a child, allowing them to struggle a little and then in a big dramatic way, let them get away and "defeat you." They get to feel themselves reclaiming their own sense of power– play is a great way to help them achieve this.

Have your kids plan some fun nights…you'll be amazed at what they come up with!

Make them think…post a social question at the beginning of the week and have a debate later in the week.

Think "outside the box" and not just going out…that's "canned fun." We want to find new and playful ways of connecting with minimum distractions.

Keeping in mind, playfulness is an attitude…it can be five minutes of hearty play and it'll do the trick. You can spend an evening, weekend or a night. The point of playful parenting is finding ways to connect over and over again. When we connect with our kids, we intuitively know what it is they need. When we step back and look at ways of fostering this through play, ideas come. If they do not, ask your child.

The whole point of play is to establish and maintain a connection. The more you play, the stronger the connection is and the less "missed-behaviors" that occur. But missed-behaviors do occur. Parenting is like driving a car. Most of us have read a manual or two and have an understanding of how to make it work. But, we want to do more than "just make it work." We want to parent on purpose and not just meander down the highway aimlessly. Play becomes the fuel that keeps our engines humming. It sustains us and allows us to go where we want to go. The regulatory system (which is the navigation system and the break) then becomes the next part of our "working car" or purposeful parenting system. I call this system Conscious Parenting Strategies (CPS).

Play Journal

Suggestion: Just like you might keep a "food journal" recording everything you eat for an entire week to take an objective view at your food consumption, keep a play journal or a journal that records how your child is spending their time for a week.

1. How many hours a day is my child sleeping?
2. How many hours a day is my child at school/doing homework?
3. How many hours does my child have structured activities (baseball, gymnastics, dance, etc.)?
4. How many hours a day is my child using something with an on/off switch (DS, computer, phone, I-pod etc.)?
5. How many hours a day is my child getting large-body (unstructured) movement (riding a bike, running, jumping, hanging from the monkey bars, swinging)?
6. How many hours a day does my child have social interaction with another child that is unstructured?
7. How many hours a day does my child have "nothing" to do where they can just play or make something out of nothing?

Activity	Sun	Mon	Tues	Wed	Thurs	Fri	Sat
Sleep							
School/ Homework							
Structured Activity							
On/Off Switch							
Large Body Movement							
Social Interaction							
"Nothing"							

You are worried about seeing him spend his early years in doing nothing. What!

Is it nothing to be happy? Nothing to skip, play, and run around all day long?

Never in his life will he be so busy again.

~Jean-Jacques Rousseau, Emile, 1762

Chapter 2 - CPS

Parenting On Purpose

A Comprehensive Plan
For Parenting With
Compassion, Patience and Simplicity
(Principles from the Tao te Ching)

When a child is first born, the top part of the hourglass is full and thus the process of parenting begins. We slowly, over time allow the sands of responsibility and learning to sift through to the child so that when they are ready to go explore the world…they truly can "own" their choices and be responsible for themselves. If this is done slowly and steadily, it is a seamless and flawless transition. To do this consciously and "on purpose" creates a well-balanced, grounded and "monster-proof" child.

I begin with an example of why I personally choose to parent consciously. It is a lesson my children have taught me over and over again. One day, my daughter and I arrived at school a little late. I was rushing her and told her to "hurry up." She stopped, looked me square in the eye, with hand on hip and said, "Mom, take a deep breathe. We don't need to hurry. Remember, we are always on time." Here's the thing. I have never really spoken these words TO my daughter, as in -- a teaching moment. I have just spoken them aloud when I am feeling stressed or rushed. My mantra is "I am always where I need to be. I am always on time" in situations like this. Today, I had forgotten! But the point is, while I was living consciously and on purpose, she was watching, learning, assimilating and remembering (and spitting it back out to me when I needed to hear it!). Oh, and to accentuate her point, when we arrived at the door where the children were going in, we literally met her teacher and her class there! Right on time!

48

C.P.S.

Conscious Parenting Strategies
Also (Compassion, Patience & Simple)
from the Tao te Ching.

While we try to teach our children all about life,
Our children teach us what life is all about.
Angela Schwindt

Conscious parenting strategies (CPS) – what does this mean? Ironically, the letters are the same for Child Protective Services. This gives those words whole new meaning! Well, let me start by explaining what it does *not* mean. This is not a parenting style such as permissive, authoritarian or authoritative. You are probably aware of these styles and the preferred (based on piles of research) method is one of authoritative. This is an unconditionally loving environment where the parents are very involved, are attentive and autonomy granting. There is a wonderful child-parent bond filled with respect and parents have reasonable expectations and have firm, loving boundaries. Ten out of ten children recommend this! It fulfills the bequeath for our children to "give them roots AND wings."

CPS presumes a basis for parenting that is respectful, unconditionally loving and grants autonomy already in place. If you are looking for further information to cultivate this foundation, one of my favorite books of all times (written in 1965, no less!) is Dr. Haim Ginott's,

Between Parent and Child. [12] It is a quick read and to me should be the handbook that comes home with every parent from the hospital! It is the foundation by which conscious parenting is built upon.

But, CPS takes this a step further. It is not just about the environment one creates that fosters a healthy self-esteem and an "I can do it!" attitude (known as self-efficacy). This is about parenting on purpose - consciously, not by default. It is not so much looking at the mundane tasks of parenting ("teach your baby to read", potty-training, discipline for toddlers), although some of things are integrated into CPS, but it is an *awareness* and *mindfulness* in parenting that looks at the long-term objective, not just the steps along the way. It is based on the Tao te Ching concepts of living, which are a constant state of **C**ompassion (unconditionally loving), with **P**atience (this is a playful connectedness that permits all feelings) and **S**implicity (less is more). It seems a good way to approach parenting as well.

It takes the concept of playful parenting (from Chapter 1), respectful parenting and kicks it all up a notch. It is about the space we as parents create and the intention of what we are nurturing within our children. The word parent comes from the Latin word, parentem, which means to "bring forth." With parenting on purpose, we are astutely aware of that which we want to "bring forth" from our child.

When it comes to kids, I like taking the child's perspective. Mostly, I think it is because children tend to be very honest, forthright and tend not to have hidden agendas. If they are hurt, they cry. If they are mad, you usually don't have to guess. But, also they are clear about their needs but not always clear about how to get those needs met.

Getting "behind the eyes of the child" has taken me into interesting (and innovative) places. When my son was diagnosed with autism, I joined a group of mothers with children who had autism. This was 16 years ago and not much about autism was known, so it was like the "cure of the month club" with so many different alternatives for treatment. It was exhausting researching each one and sometimes daunting when some of the "experts" proclaimed that, "THIS IS THE CURE!" It was easy to lose one's sense of direction (or inner voice) with this type of mindset. One particular issue with autism that experts have a strong voice about is the concept of "stimming." This self-stimulatory behavior is highly discouraged and as a matter of fact a lot of the interventions are about *stopping* this behavior. In my "not-so-like-everyone-else" thoughts, I thought, well, maybe this behavior means something. I went against the "norm" to discover what it meant.

When my son would rock back and forth clutching his arms around himself, I knew there was something inside of him that needed this type of behavior. In other words, (gasp), it served a purpose. As I did more and more research, I realized his vestibular and proprioceptive systems (which create a sense of balance and groundedness) were off. When I addressed the systems that were off at the core level, the "stimming" behavior stopped. Imagine that. He was trying to communicate a need to me. Thank God I was listening. Not with my ears. But, with my heart. That is what parenting on purpose using CPS does. It connects and listens and watches with unconditional love. It moves into action from this still space, even if it means going against what everyone else is telling you to do.

As a side note, in "listening" to my heart and my son, I was able to find solutions to what was going on with him. At 21, he is now indistinguishable from his peers and autistic-free! He just finished his second year of college! "Our story" is a book in and of itself, but suffice it to say, parenting on purpose played a lead role in his wellness!

My philosophy is that ALL behavior is a language. It is a way of communicating when you either a) can't communicate or b) do not articulate it (or maybe do not even know what it is you are trying to articulate). Think of a time when you have been upset. What kinds of "behavior" do you have (that perhaps viewed without a known "cause" might seem, well, odd)? You avoid phone calls, don't text someone back that you are mad at, storm out of a room or drink your wine straight from the bottle. The point is your behavior is communicating. It should not be a punishable offense.

When our children exhibit behaviors that are less than desirable, when we parent on purpose, we assume the best possible reason for this behavior. When we see missed-behavior as behavior that denotes "missing" something (food, or sleep) or an over-stimulating environment, expectations of adults higher than the is child capable of achieving, or just overwhelmed with an emotion, we can go about resolving the underlying issue. I look at temporary missed-behaviors like a cold, or a virus. They are an indication that something is temporarily out of alignment. We can rectify this usually very quickly and simply. But we must diagnose the underlying cause (feeling) and not just treat the symptom (behavior).

When children chronically "miss-behave," (as in missing the mark) we have a bigger illness on our hands. We need to step back and look *more* carefully at what is underneath this. Usually, we have a suspicion, (the child is overbooked, under-rested, has a poor dietary or exercise habit, too much TV/computer/video games, not enough "doing nothing" time…etc.). Sometimes taking a break from it all to see if we can find out what is wrong is all it takes to re-prioritize for our child (and ourselves). Sometimes, we will look and "find" something buried (sadness, unresolved hurts and angers) that when released allow the child to flourish once again.

It helps to view missed-behaviors like illnesses. What our children need is **C**ompassion, **P**atience and **S**implicity. We couple this underlying consciousness or mind-set with understanding and unconditional love and now we are on our way to "bringing forth" a whole being. Sometimes kids just need a prescription for vitamin PQ (peace & quiet) where they can actually utter the words, "I'm bored." We're a hurried society. No one needs to hear that anymore but we do need to be aware when we are parenting on purpose to have time when "nothing" is the order of the day. After all, to create a masterpiece, we need to start with a blank canvas.

> ## *Guidelines for Conscious Parenting*
> ## *Strategies (CPS)*

Qualities of CPS:

1. Say what you mean, mean what you say. (But, filter this through the lens of "If someone said this to me, how would it make me feel?").
2. Less is more (use less words – especially the younger the child).
3. Accept all feelings.
4. Actively listen.
5. Use "I messages" to communicate how you feel.
6. Be your child's mirror and great memory keeper.
7. Do the unexpected.

Make sure your words have meaning. How many times have you heard (or even said), "If you do that one more time?" (When it is like the 10th time they have done the thing?) "No Boundary Parenting" is scary (both for the children and those of us at the affects of it!) You would not let your child run recklessly next to a busy highway. Kids do not feel safe with parents who do not say what they mean and mean what they say.

So, what do you do if your kids do not listen to you, now? No more talking. You need to act, but with awareness – **C**ompassion, **P**atience and **S**implicity. My son used to scream when we would go to the store if he did not get a toy. It was part of the obsessive-compulsive disorder tendencies from autism, but as we were working through this behavior at a particular time, this needed to be addressed. I specifically planned for three times when I knew I could leave the store. I hired a babysitter for my older child, so that I could take my son by himself. I "set up" a situation where he would scream for a toy, couldn't have it and then leave. I just picked him up and said, "No toy today." We left. He screamed and I would just hold him in the car until he calmed down. We stayed connected. He felt loved. I wasn't frustrated because I was parenting on purpose. I KNEW it was a problem and I was taking measures to address it (instead of during my weekly grocery runs when I HAD to get food, which would have been incredibly frustrating for all concerned!) But, after doing this twice, by the third time, he accepted the words (he knew I meant it) and we were able to now shop without incident. On occasion, he would be able to get a toy, but I would let him know in advance if that were the case. My words had meaning and he knew it. But he also knew that no matter what, he was still connected to me and loved unconditionally. If I had parented "unconsciously" most likely it would have ended in a battle, frustration, probably not being able to get everything I really needed at the store and probably tears (his and mine). But, the worst part of all would be that he would have felt "conditional love" and disconnected from me. It happens when we are frustrated and unconscious. The point is to move towards greater and greater awareness of what we are "bringing forth."

Unconditionally loving means no matter what - "I love you". It does not mean a "Walk all over me" sign is on your forehead. If you were driving down Highway 1 in California where there are pretty much cliffs on either side, would you feel safe if there were no guardrails? Where would you drive? I am pretty sure it'd be down the middle of the road, weaving back and forth. This is what our children do when they do not have healthy "guardrails" which are the boundaries we set up. We do this with words that convey, "I say what I mean and mean what I say. I love you no matter what **and** you are safe to drive in your own lane".

We are all very creative and resourceful. We just have to be aware of 1) if there is a problem and 2) what it is. Then, we can move into action. Most likely we are pretty aware of it. Now, we just need to create a plan to lovingly and consciously - "on purpose", find a solution. Sometimes, we have to get pretty innovative.

Less is more. Do you ever wonder if when we start pontificating to our children if we don't sound like the squawky Charlie Brown schoolteacher? We generally talk too much to our children. I do - and I observe it all around. I believe our intentions are good and we explain to the nth degree. But, really, there are times when we just need to stop talking. For instance, pointing and saying "Dishes" (when they are left on the table) or "Shoes" when they are on the floor, or just "No" and walk away.

I also find saying "yes" is very easy most of the time. Hear me out - this is not about giving in to every request. But, how often do we say no, when "Yes, later" could be an option? "Can I have a cookie?"

57

("Yes, after dinner" – if that is actually acceptable). Or "Can I have this toy?" (Yes…you have a birthday coming up, let's write it down (I always carry a notebook for things like this – it lets the child know that they are heard). Or…hmm…let's write it down and if you really want it, we'll find out some jobs you can do to earn it. One thing children need to learn for developmental reasons is delayed gratification.

On that note, as an aside, a study was conducted by Walter Mischel where children had one marshmallow in front of them and were told they would be given a second one if they could wait. This study was conducted when the children were four and a follow-up on test scores when the children were 18. The children who were able to delay gratification and wait for the second marshmallow were significantly more competent and had higher SAT scores by 210 points![13] Teaching children to wait is a conscious parenting thing to do. It's hard and they will try to wear us down. But, we must be strong. Their healthy development depends on it!

The more words we use the more it sounds like we're trying to justify ourselves and also the more "wiggle" room for those clever children to hold your words against you. Parenting on purpose with CPS is about connecting and loving unconditionally. We foster connectedness when we respect our child's ability to hear what we said, understand it and accept it. If they show feelings of resistance, it is a good time to show unconditional love, ("It's hard." Administered with understanding and feeling and a hug that connects and affirms your love.)

Working with my son and the developmentally delayed population, I learned an important lesson about communicating. Less truly is more. First of all, children have short attention spans and "short" short-term memories. Sometimes, children have undiagnosed auditory processing disorders and they literally do not hear all of what you are saying. A healthy, well-balanced, with no challenges, four-year-old can hold about four "bits" of information at once. What this means is if you told them to do four things in sequence and then had them go do it, most likely they could do that. The key here is "most likely". There are many things to be distracted with when you are four! But, when you have sentences with more than four bits of information, you have now overloaded the system. Most likely they will hear a few things, like the last thing you said.

When we add to this any type of deficiency such as being tired, hungry, distracted or just simply an, "I just don't wanna do it" attitude, the child can hold even less information. Children with auditory processing issues are even more challenged to retain information. To make the most of your "less is more" conversations, first, get eye contact, use fewer words and if possible, pair with a visual cue. It is helpful to have a child repeat back to you what they heard. In addition, it is best to tell a child what you want, not what you do not want. "Please color on paper" instead of "Do not color on the walls."

One other aspect of the "less is more" concept in CPS (simplicity) is looking at toys, games, movies and activities that our child is engaged in. This is not meant to be an overwhelming issue, but it is worth mentioning. When parenting on purpose, we want to look at all aspects of our "bringing forth" role and be sure we are bringing forth what we want. I'm pretty sure none of us want to create hoarders, video game champions or stressed out, overbooked children. We do not have to overhaul the whole system, today, all at once. We just want to parent on purpose and be aware of areas that could use a little more simplification. Before each birthday and Christmas, my kids and I would go through their toys, books and clothes. We had three boxes: "Keep", "Donate", and "Save for six months". If the "Six Month" box was not even mentioned during the six month period, it would be donated at the end of six months. It has worked beautifully at our house. We also try to release something when we get something new. I do this myself. When I get a new pair of shoes, I donate a pair I have (and this is hard because I really do love shoes!) Enough said. ☺

Accept all feelings. It sounds so simple, doesn't it? But, invariably, there is one (or more) that may be difficult for us to take in. How often do you find yourself saying, "Don't feel bad. Here's a cookie (or whatever)" or "Stop crying. It's just a scratch." Or "It was just a doll, you have a bunch. We'll get a new one." Imagine anyone of these things said to you by your spouse over the loss of something important. Ouch. Sometimes our children's feelings make us uncomfortable. Sometimes, they are just inconvenient, and so they "feel" insignificant. To us.   Sometimes it is because it reminds us of feelings we have that are not-so-pleasant and we don't want to deal with. For most women, the feeling is anger. Research shows that we tolerate anger from boys more, and sadness less and just the opposite for girls. It is not healthy and we need to address it. When we are consciously parenting, we always keep in mind, "How would this feel if said to me?" (Again, you have to kick it up a notch for it to be meaningful. You might not care if your ice cream fell on the floor, but what if you lost your diamond ring down the drain?) We want to connect. We do this and show this by what we say (or don't say). Perspective taking is a very important part of conscious parenting.

Pausing to take a moment to really see and feel what our child is experiencing allows us to really connect, makes loving unconditionally very easy and then the solution arises quite simply.

Using the concept that less is more, we try to match the feeling with as few as words as possible. Our child will let us know if we're on track or not. "Ouch!" "It hurts." "It's hard to lose something we love." "Wow.   You are mad about that!"   Letting the feeling come, acknowledging it and allowing the child to feel through it (having been heard and validated) is so healing (for both the child and us).

 I was at the store and a child had fallen down and was wailing. The mother was trying everything to coerce the child out of her feelings, understandably so – it was quite the noise. I was walking by and just said, "Ouch. That hurts." The little girl looked up at me with such relief, like someone understood, immediately stopped crying and got up and was completely over it. The mother looked at me like I was either an angel or a witch. Not sure. But, she smiled and thanked me and we all went about our days. The point is kids are smart. They know what they feel and are not afraid to feel it and make us face it or feel uncomfortable in the process. I think that's why I love them so much! They are real and force us to be so as well... teenagers, in particular. They "buck" the system, question authority and make us all examine ourselves more closely. It is uncomfortable if you don't care much for introspective thinking and growing. It's "miracle grow" if you do.

When we understand how the brain works (see next chapter for more details on this!) it helps us to "connect" with the part of the brain our child is operating out of.

As we utilize CPS in our parenting, we learn to accept all feelings. Amazingly, we learn to accept our own feelings as well and this is a very freeing feeling! When we see our feelings as a temperature gauge for where we are at, we learn to read it better in ourselves and our children. When we are aware, we are much more capable of responding appropriately.

Actively Listen. H.E.A.R. your child – (Have Empathy – Accurately Respond). I love the line in Avatar where Mo'at (Nyteri's mother) says, "It is impossible to fill a cup that is already full." This has many meanings. But, when your child's cup is filled with emotions, nothing else is going to get in. We have to empty the cup of the raw emotion that is there and we do this by actively listening. We do this by being fully present with our *whole* being to really hear what is being communicated (either in words or by behavior). Have you ever had a conversation with someone who really listened, I mean with their whole being? Very few of us have these interactions (unless we pay a therapist to do this for us). Listening is an acquired skill. When one listens, actively, very few words are spoken. We look for "cues" or unspoken things. Most of a child's behavior is communicating, while very rarely are the words the clue to what is going on. It is amazing what a "plugged in" response will do for a child (and an adult for that matter!) To have someone really hear and understand you and acknowledge what you are feeling is liberating. So, listen with the intention of connecting to your child and what they are experiencing.

I like to ask myself the question when I am listening to my child (or anyone for that matter), "Am I adding to the problem or lessoning and moving toward a solution?" For example, my child says, "I hate so and so." If I am adding to the problem, I begin a lesson, "Wow, hate is such a strong word, don't you mean dislike?" This adds to the problem, because I am not listening, I am getting distracted by the "symptoms" and not the problem.

What is the real problem? My kid has some very strong feelings (who cares about the words right now?) about this situation. To lesson the problem or move toward a solution (a child who has had his feelings heard and thus feels loved and "connected") I say, "Wow! You are REALLY angry about this huh?" This opens the door for more communication and creates a space where "spilling more of their cup" becomes safe. The more we do this, the more they spill. This becomes our saving grace during adolescence. We have built up a "history" of accepting spillage and they know they are safe, connected and loved enough to spill out even their not-so-great feelings. And my philosophy is better out than in.

I like using a telephone conversation as an example of good technique. First of all, you have to make sure you are "dialed in" and have the right number. Make sure you are connecting with the right feeling. When we say, "Wow you are angry about that." We are dialing a number. If it's the wrong number, our child will let us know, then we "re-dial" and make sure we are connected.

Next, one person talks at a time (usually our child). Then, we clarify (make sure you are hearing what they said accurately). When we are actively listening, we are always making sure we are "connected". When our child spills more information out of their cup, "Suzie called me a poopy head." Sometimes we clarify (but we don't' want to parrot, that's annoying) and sometimes we nod our heads or say, "Ouch. Or, " Tell me more." When the conversation is over, we allow the child to "end" the conversation. When they have adequately "spilled" out their cup, you'll probably see a smile or a recognition that they are done.

Sometimes our children express things about themselves that are hard to hear. "I am ugly." Often, this might trigger some insecurities in our own being or bring up unresolved hurts. We need to pause and check in with ourselves to make sure we are not adding to the problem by mixing our own stuff with our child's. Sometimes, we want to rush in and argue with them (adding to the problem) because we don't want our child to feel bad about themselves. But, we must remember, this is our *child's* experience right now. We don't have to agree with them. But to lesson the problem, we acknowledge what they are feeling, "Wow, that can feel really bad to feel like that." "Tell me more." We can also say, "I know this might not help, but I don't see you that way." But, if a child is permitted to feel what they feel and spill out their cup, then they will be ready to re-fill with goodness. Active listening creates awareness for us on when to let spill and when to re-fill. The more we do it, the more in-tune we get with this flow.

"From a mirror we want an image, not a sermon." Haim Ginott

When we seek to be a mirror for our child, we seek stillness. We find this by being silent and present. We listen and allow. Something I learned about communicating with my autistic son was many times I had to "wait for it." This skill has been a huge asset in my other communications. We are, as a society, not very comfortable with silence, so it takes some getting used to. But, it works and it is powerful. When we are silent and fully present, our children know it! Try waiting just a few more minutes before replying when your child talks. Take slow, long deep breaths and really try to connect with where they are "at". Often, when we are about to speak, just that little bit of an opening allows the child to spill out what is really hurting them. Don't be afraid to wait for it.

Use "I" messages to communicate. It has taken me a while to realize that not everyone experiences the world the way I do (including my children!) I know this sounds ridiculous but we often assume that everyone can see things the same way we do. They don't. So, speaking from the perspective of "I" becomes a useful tool in communication. Whenever we use the word "you" in a sentence, it generally is in an attack mode. Now, we might not mean this, but generally it is taken that way from our children and then we are not going to elicit the cooperation or connection that we are seeking. Hear the difference in these two approaches to the same problem, "You never clean up your room. It is so messy. You have clothes and toys all over the floor." Or, "I feel frustrated when I try to come in your room and have no place to walk." I communicate my feelings and give her an opportunity to correct it – without launching into attack mode. If my child chooses not to, I can say, "I cannot come into your room when it is a mess. It feels unsafe to me. But, I am happy to talk to you out in the hallway." What is interesting is that most of us would not ever use "You" language when talking to a friend or a guest, but we do it quite often with those we love.

What is so great about using "I" messages is that we can always be congruent with our words. We do not have to pretend to be patient when we are clearly NOT. (This is very confusing to a child when our behavior does not match our words…said through gritted teeth, "I'M FINE!") Instead, we can say, "I have the patience the size of a pea right now." All the feelings, none of the guilt from having exploded at some point all over the place because we're trying to keep the lid on so tight! Part of our conscious parenting is making sure we are compassionate, patience and simplistic with *ourselves*, too. Although most of us have an "S" (as in Super-human!) metaphorically tattooed on our chests because of all of the ways in which we do what we do, it is important to allow ourselves our feelings, too.

What's great about communicating feelings from *our* perspective is that it truly is the only perspective we CAN have. We also move from a place of "I am the adult telling you how to think, feel and behave" to "I am respecting you as an individual, telling you how I feel and trusting you to figure out what to do." It has been my experience, the more respect and trust a child is given, the more they give back. Having seen a child who was told what to do, what to wear and how to think until about age 13, I saw the detrimental affects this had, even into early adulthood. She might have been listening because she didn't have a choice and blindly obeying when she was younger, but, guess who she started listening to during adolescence? On the other side, seeing a child that was given choices, allowed the opportunity to make mistakes and correct them (or live with the consequences) and seeing how this young person grew into a responsible, thinking adult makes a difference. When a child is given a voice (but has learned boundaries and respect too) they do not give away their personal power during adolescence.

One last thought about communication. When we are actively listening, using "I" messages to communicate, we are being present and aware. We are not parenting by default. This is truly conscious parenting. Another way to communicate consciously is to state the facts. "I see a messy room" (no judgment, allows the child to figure it out). Also, when our child cleans the room, we don't' praise them. We state what we see. "Wow this room was so messy and look at it now!" (Our child gets to allow the sense of accomplishment well up inside of *them*, "Yea, I cleaned it!") We state, "Clothes put away, books on shelf – wow!" Our child, "I did it all by myself!" Us, "High 5." They begin to do things for the sake of doing them and how it makes them feel (not seeking a dangling carrot – our approval and praise). Our love should be unconditional and overflowing into their cups non-stop. When we communicate like this, it allows our child to do (even when no one is looking) the things they need to do. This is how life really works. We have to have an internal push to drive us toward doing what it is we are to do. We won't always have someone there to offer us toys, cookies or praise to do things. We want to transfer (sands through the hourglass) the sense of accomplishment and the feelings of goodness that come from completing a job to our child as early as we can. We can share in their exuberance at their independence and accomplishments, but our love and adoration should be free-flowing and independent of anything, I repeat, *anything* our child does.

This type of languaging allows for us to address things when their behavior is not optimal. We can still speak into that with a sense of autonomy and balance. We state the facts as we see them and how we feel about it or how it affects us and then give our child the opportunity to fix it. Having a conscious strategy when things go "wrong" is a great tool. We stlll get to stay connected and foster the unconditional love we have for our child.

Be your child's mirror and memory keeper. Did you know that fifty percent of your brain is dedicated to vision? We are visual creatures. Pictures make visual impressions. Especially for younger children and for those who have difficulty processing auditorily (which there are a lot of these). When you want your child to repeat a behavior (brushing their teeth, cleaning their room, etc.) snap a picture. Put it up. When they have a good experience, have them "tap in the joy" by taking their middle finger and tapping three times in between their eyebrows while smiling. Make a list of things your child does that you like or that requires extra effort. When they are discouraged or need a reminder, remind them of the time they were successful. I recommend a bucket that your child decorates and then have them continually fill their bucket with their accomplishments and things they do that they are proud of – or a large poster that they can hang up and see everyday.

Also, when things are difficult, have your "list" of their accomplishments in your mind to remind them of how they have succeeded. "Wow, this reminds me of the time you climbed Camelback Mountain. Do you remember how hard that was? You were only 8 years old?" See their little face lights up with the feeling of *their* accomplishment and it reminds them of their abilities to overcome difficult situations. You can also have them create an "I can do anything" journal or jar, where they list their prior accomplishments that they can look at when feeling overwhelmed with a new task. That is why it is so important to give them ownership over their accomplishments early on (why praise backfires...a child figures out very quickly with praise that it is a two-edged sword...whereas, accomplishments are theirs alone). But, as mirrors, we must reflect back accurately our child's feelings, but also their true essence. It is easy to forget this and there will be many people (especially at school) who will try to distort your child's view of themselves. Many children growing up today have very empty cups. They are seeking to fill them, but usually at other children's expenses. It is most likely the cause of rampant bullying. You cannot give away what you do not have inside. Children, who are empty, sad, and defeated, give away emptiness, sadness (usually in the form of verbal "vomit" or worse) and defeating behaviors. Our kids need mirrors now more than anything.

70

Do the unexpected. When you do the unexpected – expect to make an impact. Let's face it, we're all way too predictable. Our kids can usually repeat what we're going to say before we say it. We become this background hum to their daily lives. The point with conscious parenting – is we are parenting on purpose. We take the role of "teacher" seriously and want to teach more than just really great tuning-out skills. I remember one particularly frustrating day when every one of the four kids in my house were whining. There was nothing in particular that was "wrong" – just you know, the certain pitch that only dogs hear! I had had it. But, instead of my usual lecture, I went to the answering machine, pushed the "record outgoing message" and proceeded to say the following: "You have reached WHINE-11, please leave your message (to which I screeched AFTER THE BEEP! It was a performance befitting of an Oscar! I nailed it!). I then went to my room for a nice soak. The kids had a great laugh over this and amazingly they were all still living (and actually productive) when I re-emerged. Even funnier, my friend had called and left a message during my de-briefing in the bathtub and got a nice laugh, too! The point is, sometimes, you just gotta play it a little Zen-like "koan-think'in" crazy. A lecture would have fallen on deaf ears. Their "whines" were not productive. Later, we were able to talk and laugh and process all of the little things that were going on. But, "in the meantime" – which is of course where we live most of our lives, we "crazied" it up a bit and it worked. I have been known to "crazy" it up a bit to make a point. It sure beats the same old drone of talking

71

(especially with older kids), it is playful and allows your kids to see a "real live person in there" and they remember it.

For example, if you want to make a point about how we make things more difficult than we have to sometimes, have a night where everyone tries to eat dinner with their non-dominant hand. Or try to tie your shoes with gloves on, or blindfold your child and have him try to walk through the house. Another thing I used to do with my kids is to show them how we can make things "difficult" and miserable by being very demonstrative. I'll spill the blocks all over the place and grumble and dramatically pick them up and make a big production of it, moaning, whining, fussing and carrying on. They would love this production – it caught their attention. Then, I'll stand up, act as if I've had a life-changing experience, pop in some fun music and start shooting baskets with the blocks in the bucket – dancing and having fun. Another thing I have done is to give my kids a bucket with a hole in it. I'll ask them to fill it up with water. They will giggle at how ridiculous as the water keeps coming out. It is a good demonstration that sometimes we have "holes" in our lives and how we try to fill them up, but they keep leaking out. The point is about all of these things is that they make an impression and teach a lesson without words, usually. That's what I love about Zen – it's often ridiculous, but the child will learn the lesson in their own way with you acting "a fool" (and hopefully having fun in the process -- I know I do!). It seems the best and most meaningful lessons we have are learned on our own, but also through a happy heart-doorway. Sometimes the lessons through the back-door (while consciously delivered) allow for the greatest learning, because the child "gets it" for themselves…they connect the dots. We just put the dots really close together and make a ridiculously memorable picture.

So… what do we do when things get a little bumpy?

There are two processes I like to employ. The first is called **Stop, Drop & Roll** (yea, like – someone is one fire here!). The second is a **Speed B.U.M.P**.

Stop, Drop & Roll – I love this because we all know this is what we are to do when we are on fire and I can't think of anything that "heats us up" more than a child mis-behaving. And they are oh-so-good at timing this!

Stop – stop what you are doing. Breathe. Slow. Through your nose.

Drop – not only to your knees (prayer-pose always a good thing), but at eye level, looking into your child's eyes and then continue to "drop" your breath down a notch…when the fire has stopped coming out of your nostrils you know you have achieved a responsive breath. For older kids, you don't need to drop to your knees, but drop into a memory of them that opens your heart chakra and lets love in. Conjure up a memory of your child that makes you melt (my "go to memory" of my daughter is with her shoes on the wrong feet...how cute is that? And it always brings me back) and it will open up your heart for conscious action.

Roll – you can roll around on the floor with them, playfully of course, if you are in the mood for that...but the point is to roll with the energy – remember energy moves...jump up and down with them...forget about everyone and everything around you and connect – that's all they really want and need right now. They are out-of-control and need someone to remind them how to come back to center and that no matter what they are loved and safe. They are using their reptilian brain (more on this later), so they will not be able to take in what you are saying. Match your breath to theirs and try slowing it down a bit. Let them know you see them and hear them. **Use very few words.** This is important. If you notice EMTs and firefighters don't talk a lot during a crisis. There's a reason for this. If you do talk, use few words and speak slowly and quietly. Connect with where they are at...if it is still going on, move onto the "Speed Bump" (below) technique.

Don't be discouraged.

It's often the last key in the bunch that opens the lock.

Author unknown

Speed Bump – Speed bumps serve to slow us down. So, when we have a problem or encounter a "mis-behavior", I like to ask the following questions. 1) (**B**) – **Basic needs** – are they being met (are they tired, hungry, over-stimulated etc.?) Many times this one slips right by us as we drag our oh-so-exhausted two-year-old to a lunch he doesn't want to go to, in a place he has no interest in being at, at a time when his body should be sleeping. It happens and we have to go with it, sometimes – but a little awareness in this situation goes a long way for easing stressed out two-year olds. 2) (**U**) – **Understand** – do I truly understand what is going on and are my expectations realistic? 3) (**M**) – **Matter** – will this matter in 5 (5 minutes, 5 days or 5 years) – how important is what is going on? 4) (**P**) – **Problem** – whose problem is this? Is it my problem? Have I created unrealistic expectations? Or is it my child's problem? My problem would be clothes (or dishes or insert any thing lying around your house) strewn on my living room floor...the child does not "own" the problem...because they do not care (this is different from taking responsibility for the problem). It is "my problem" because I don't want it here.

This does not mean I need to take responsibility for rectifying the problem. I have two choices. I can use my "I message" to communicate that this is unacceptable. I can also (depending on how much I want to be at peace) deal with it. There are combinations therein (sometimes, I deal with it, sometimes I let my child know the effect it has on me (leaves me tired and frustrated and less energy to do fun things with them, or not feeling a desire to take them out to a movie or pizza when I have to spend my time and energy picking up after them).

When we are clear about who owns the problem, we can be clear who gets to resolve it. It does not mean we will not ever again have conflicts. It just means when we do, we get clear about what the conflict is, who "owns" it and communicate with effective "I" messages what we are thinking and feeling.

Sometimes, kids need a place to go to pull things together. "Time out" is not necessarily effective unless the child is able to actually understand and "re-think" or as I like to say, think a new thought. I created a safe space where my kids could go when they had calmed down from a TANTrum – they can go to the T.A.N.T. (think a new thought) chair. (It is important that the child does not feel unloved or dis-connected, so sometimes, holding them in this place until they choose something to help in the re-direction of thought). You can also create "The Peaceful Place". I like a big bean bag chair with a basket of things to allow for new thoughts – blank paper/crayons, maybe an iPod or mp3 player with some calming music, a cuddly bear to hang onto, calming activities to do. The point is that your child needs something/s to facilitate thinking new thoughts. (We can't solve the problem with the same mind that created it...so, creating a new thought might require some creation space). We do this when we take a bath, read a book, take a walk, etc. Just "sitting" in a chair excommunicated from their Source of love (us) will only lead to more "missed" behaviors. Especially when the "time in" (the time they spend with us) they do not feel unconditionally loved and accepted.

When the child is ready to get up ask them 1) Why are you here? And 2) What can you do differently next time? The point of this exercise is to think new thoughts and to grow in understanding of how our behavior affects us. These questions might be difficult at first and might require some prompting. But, this is not about shame or guilt. It is all part of our quest to facilitate thinking and reasoning in our children. As we will look more closely at during the "Mind" section of this book, the prefrontal cortex is our "thinking brain". We want to exercise and nurture this part of the brain as much as possible. Our kids learn through trial and error.

Thomas Edison was asked if he considered the numerous times he failed in an attempt to make a light bulb a failure. He replied, "No, I just found 1,099 ways NOT to make a light bulb. In order for our children to learn ways in which to "be" in this world, they might need a few (times a few) of how NOT to be in this world. Life is mostly experiential – especially for kids.

But, we also need to make sure we have realistic expectations of behaviors for our children. I have observed countless situations where children are where they just shouldn't be. I understand why they are there, I have been there. But, as a rule, dragging a two-year-old child out to dinner at 8:00 p.m. at night is a recipe for disaster. The point of

CPS is *not* to parent by default. There are ways around these disasters and most of that comes from thinking through situations before they happen.

If you really have no other choice than to go out to dinner at 8:00 P.M., plan accordingly. Have a "restaurant only" bag that is filled with new things that entertain (coloring book/crayons, stickers, pocket family games to play – what a great way to "connect" with one another!). Call ahead for seating. When my son was in the throes of autism, we did not have a lot of time that he could sit at a restaurant so I needed to plan accordingly and be prepared. I used to call in our orders ahead of time. A lot of restaurants will do this. On occasion, my husband and I would drive separately, so he could arrive first, get a table and order. I'd show up with the kids, and we were able to enjoy a nice dinner out during the "window of opportunity" instead of using all that precious time up waiting in an over-crowded, hot and noisy waiting room. When we are consciously parenting, we are looking at chronic issues or problems, not just isolated "had a bad day" ones. We are seeking ways of resolving these issues consciously. We are looking at creative ways of teaching and "bringing forth" a whole child.

CPS is a little bit of work. But it is more pre-emptive work. It is thinking ahead through situations and looking at each issue that arises and seeing how you can parent consciously but also maintain the compassion, patience and simplicity concepts, not only for your child

78

but also for yourself. Most of the reason I have parented this way is because I want to be peaceful. That's right, it is selfish (or self-preservation - not sure which one). But, I wanted to enjoy my experiences as a parent and not just endure them. There are some things we do just have to endure. These are moments we breathe, give thanks for our many blessings and move through them.

But, in general, a lot of the stress we experience is a result of lack of awareness or just poor planning. When we bring something into the light, it is much easier to see what is missing or what needs to be altered to create more peace and harmony. When we create this peace and harmony within ourselves it expands out to encompass our family. Our children grow up in an environment that fosters that internal space of stillness. It is an indescribable gift. Because when the world "out there" (that they invariably get to) is whirling about, the world "in here" is calm and still. They have a center that they have grown up in, observed you consciously creating and they can move "monster-proofed" from this space.

I have saved the best for last. The last chapter discussed the importance of playful parenting. There are so many times that being playful diffuses angry, tense or yucky feelings. When I would tuck my daughter in, she had a hard time letting me go at night. I would try to go, and she would come after me, and it ended up in a battle or "If you come out one more time…" So, one night, I looked in her bed at all of the stuffed animals. I said to her, "If Mommy were one of these stuffed animals, which one would she be?" She pointed to Hello Kitty. I said (in my best British accent), "Well, hello Lisa. It looks like you will be staying here with Riley tonight." I got out of bed and Riley continued this, giggling with glee and happy that she would have "Lisa/Mommy" with her all night. It has worked every night since then. The point was in staying connected. Play was the forum that facilitated this connection.

When you are parenting consciously the **main** goal is to stay connected. When kids feel connected, they feel loved and safe. When kids feel unconditionally loved and safe they have healthy self-esteems and a strong sense of self-efficacy. This is the prescription for "monster-proofing" your child. When children are "full" of love it is all they give away and all they accept. They might still get their feelings hurt or feel sad, but their overall resiliency is one of "I can do it and I like me!" Having watched a few of my children navigate to adulthood, I can tell you that there is nothing like watching a child traverse through the perils of adolescence. It is daunting to watch helplessly from the shore as they commandeer their own ship. What is comforting is to know that amidst choppy waters, when they are "full" and know who they are, their compass always points due North and no matter what storms they encounter, they have the skills to navigate safely to the other shore.

Parenting on purpose, consciously, loving unconditionally, always. No exceptions. Staying connected, always. No exceptions. It is the gift we give our children and in turn, give ourselves.

As parents, we are **always** teaching. So, then the question becomes, "What is it that I am teaching?" It is often not what we think. We think our children learn from only what we say. However, children watch and learn mostly what we **do**. When we parent consciously, our communication (both spoken and unspoken) serves to convey our unconditional love and keep us connected. When we use our words carefully, accept all feelings, listen and communicate "on purpose" and in love our children learn that they can trust us with all their feelings. Even when we might not know what to do or what our child is trying to communicate, we connect to them in a way that communicates, that although we might not always understand what they are saying or doing, we understand *them.*

A poet once visited the court of a king who ruled in Arab lands yet knew no Arabic or Persian, only Turkish. The poet brought a beautiful eulogy to the king, but it was written, of course in Arabic. When he recited the poem, however, the king nodded at all the right places; laughed where he was supposed to; looked sad or amazed or contemplative at just the right moment. After the poet left, the king's courtiers were worried. Had the king known Arabic all along? If so, they could be in trouble for all the sarcastic asides they'd spoken to each other over the years in Arabic. They bribed the king's favorite servant to find out.

One day, when the king was in a good mood, his servant asked him straight out—did he know Arabic? If not, how did he know to respond to the poet?

"Of course I don't know Arabic," said the king. "But, I knew what the poet's purpose was. His purpose wasn't the poem, it was to impress, amuse, and entertain me. I understood him, so I didn't need to understand the poem."

With CPS we are seeking to understand our child from an unconditionally loving (accepting all feelings), connected place. When we do this, no matter what the behavior or "Arabic" they might be speaking that we do not understand, we understand them.

If we would listen to our kids,

we'd discover that they are largely self-explanatory.

Robert Brault

Helping Our Child Deal With Their Feelings

There is a form of therapy called Hakomi that is incredibly powerful. The central themes of Hakomi are: safety, loving presence, and acceptance. It is a mindful practice and very empowering as it allows the client to experience their own feelings in a "nonviolent way", in which the therapist does not impose their beliefs, observations or analyses upon the client. They use their expertise and create a space for the client to go about "self-discovery". This allows the person to discover what is right and true for them.

This is the approach we want to take when dealing with our child's feelings. When we state what we see ("I saw you slammed the door and stomped to your room.") we connect or attune with our child or we can simply state, "I noticed…" Then, we add, "Wow, something pretty bad must have happened to make you this angry." We are "dialing" in to how our child is feeling. We then get to help them process it by asking them to "name it" or give it a shape or a color. By taking a feeling (which comes from the "right brain") and giving it some type of tangible quality (which is what satisfies the "left brain"), we get integration. We can then coach our child to do something with this object. They can release it or use their magic mind wands to make it disappear. We empower them with tools to deal with what they are feeling with words and tools.

There is something that happens in our brains when we feel empathy. When we feel empathy, a strong resonance happens between us and the other person. It begins with mirror neurons and echoes throughout all the pathways, creating a sense of softening and relaxation in the body. [14] When we feel this and continually tap into this, we truly are able to create a loving, safe space for our child.

Little children can "color" their feelings or use "tear art" to create something out of all their feelings or use puppets or dolls. Giving the "story" an outlet allows the child to process all of the pieces and parts that are jumbled up into something that makes sense.

This process can take a few minutes or a few days, depending on what the child is dealing with. But, when we help them sort it out, we are giving them incredible tools!

Moving their bodies is an important part of processing feels, too. If we can have them focus on where they "feel" the emotion in their body and see if they can find clever ways of moving the energy up and out their fingers or "stomp" it our of their feet, it is very helpful.

As human beings, we have a natural tendency to organize ourselves. As we become more aware and mindful, we can place attention and gather insight to make our actions in life more effective. We teach our children how to do this as well. Our children are not born innately knowing how to handle their emotions. We teach them by providing feedback and insight. We can tell them what we notice ("I noticed you seemed _____"). They will let us know if we are accurate, but it does bring their current emotional state to their awareness. Then, they can be mindful of what they are feeling, place attention on it, and then you can gather insight to allow for processing and a more efficient way of being in life. This requires no more skill than the powers of observation, free of an opinion. When you notice, you simply state what you see. The child will fill in the blanks and you simply help them name what they are feeling so that they can begin to process it outside of themselves.

A very important part of helping children deal with their feelings and regulate their emotions is to emphasize the power of their thoughts to create and change their perceptions and their world. Helping children "reframe" concepts about themselves and beliefs they have can dramatically change their worlds. Teaching them to smile and laugh will change their brain chemistry. Research shows that smiling can help produce more serotonin, the "feel good" chemical in the brain. Try humor with your child and being playful (when appropriate) about life. Sharing a similar experience with your child can help them see that even adults struggle with life and that we can process it, release it and move on with grace and hopefully a little humor.

Working Ourselves Out Of A Job

As mentioned previously, Haim Ginott wrote a very simple, yet complete book about treating a child with respect. His classic book, written in 1963, *Between Parent and Child* has been the foundation of many subsequent books. The premise of Ginott's teaching was a basic understanding of why children do what they do; that their behavior is a way of communicating.

We all want to be loved and accepted on a very core level. We do things for a reason – a payoff. It would seem counter-intuitive to misbehave for attention. But, if it's your only recourse, or you receive a greater "pay-off" (by way of response), it's what you do. We get "hard-wired" for a response – the bigger the response – the bigger the "tickler" created on the file of our brains. Many children have learned how to "miss-behavior" rather well, because it evokes the greatest response and energy from us. Children will do what is expected, but if we are "owning their problems" they have little motivation to do so for themselves.

Have you ever stopped to think about how often we own our children's problems? We own their grades, their hunger, their friendships, even if they need a sweater or not! An interesting concept is stopping and asking oneself when something comes up, "Who should really handle this?"

For instance, if your child is 6 months old and needs a jacket to stay warm, or food when hungry, or nap when tired, it's YOUR problem. You need to fix it. If your child is 16 years old and needs a sweater, food or sleep, it's THEIR problem. They will learn in just a few minutes of not wearing a sweater (being cold) what you may have tried to teach them for six months. Yet when does the transition from total dependency occur?

A little bit at a time.

When we own our problems and allow our child to own their problems, we are both empowered to resolve whatever problem is in front of us. The beauty of this for our child is that they have many opportunities to learn how to take responsibility for their choices. If a child is "always" doing something, remember – there's a payoff. Find out what the payoff is.

We cannot make our kids responsible.

We can only give them opportunities to practice responsibility. Most lessons we learn are through failed attempts. If we go hungry because we forget our lunch, or are cold because we don't bring a jacket, or get our bike stolen because we don't lock it up, we learn something. If we have someone continually bringing our lunch to school, reminding us to bring our sweater or reminding us to lock up our bike, when exactly do we learn to do this for ourselves?

Because we will at some point and time have to do this for ourselves. It's just a matter of time. Now, I am not suggesting not bringing a kindergartner his or her lunch if they forget. I mean, come on, they're 5! They're concerned about what they're bringing for Show 'N Tell! But, if a child in the sixth grade still needs woken up in the morning, his jacket handed to him on the way out the door and a lunch brought to him at school, he's not getting very prepared for the real world.

There's a hierarchy of learning and we need to get on it! We have to get the fundamentals down so that we can move on to the bigger issues. All of these "small steps" along the way add up to great growth in the prefrontal cortex (our thinking brain) and this is very important for good decision-making

We can start by asking ourselves each time something arises. "Should I really intervene here, or is there the slightest possibility my child can figure this out for themselves?"

As parents sometimes, we tend to apply our boundaries and discipline backwards. There seem to be a lot of what I like to call "boundary-less parenting" going on. These are children who have not been guided at all and do not listen under any circumstances and seem to have their parents over a barrel. Yet, when that child becomes a teenager, the parents try to enforce rules, boundaries and make their children responsible, to no avail. It's like having a puppy and letting them piddle in every room in your house. Then, when they become a full-grown dog, and you've had just about enough, you try to restrict this huge dog from all the rooms except one. It's just not going to happen. The big dogs win!

So, if your child has had boundaries and choices and consequences their *entire* existence up until now and you have fostered a friendly and respectful relationship filled with unconditional love but firm boundaries, they will have internalized this into real knowing. They have no need to rebel because you have honored their individuality and respect who they are. Again, you might not always accept their behavior, but at this point, "life" does the teaching and your child actually assimilates real-life experiences into knowledge.

I remember my daughter at 18 decided to go out with a friend and wanted me to set a pretend curfew so she could break it. She had never had a curfew, as she had been regulating her behavior, living with a few "rough" life consequences along the way and was able to self-monitor. Which, of course was a good thing as she was "legal" at this time.

I laughed and asked her why and she said, "Well, teenagers are supposed to rebel." She laughed and so did I and I set a pretend curfew (she was still in before it!) I joked with her and told her she "epically failed at being a teenager!" Again – all in good fun! She had no real need to rebel, because she had learned throughout her life that ultimately she was the one who would deal with life's consequences, not me.

It's like when she was little and I would tell her, "I'm going to say something that is totally gonna make you want to stomp your feet and slam your door." She would get so mad and say, "Now, I can't do those things!" Precisely (or in kid language, "duh!"). When you give them "permission" to do what it is you don't want them to do, it takes all the fun out of it! When there's nothing to rebel against, why rebel? Then, they can just get on to the business of figuring out who they really are and settle into that.

You've already demonstrated, "You can't scare me! Blue hair, piercings and all...underneath it all you are still you and you are the most PERFECT version of you that exists and nothing will ever change my love for you!" When those are words that the child *hears and feels* from you, under any circumstance, they'll come to you with the big stuff. If my child is about to get into a car with someone who has been drinking (or worse yet, they have been drinking) I want them to know at their very core, "I can call Mom (or Dad) without fear of rejection. There may be consequences, but our relationship will still be intact" (and so will their bodies).

Those are the moments we ultimately prepare for - or really- provide the opportunities for our child to prepare for.

Like it or not, we're working ourselves out of a job. I don't know about you, but I'd rather have my child have a lot of "on the job training" in failing and living with natural consequences, than telling them what to do their whole lives and find out when the true test comes (yea, 18 is legal), they fail miserably.

WABI-SABI Parenting
Seeing the Perfect in the Imperfect

The art of seeing the perfect in the imperfect is an ancient Chinese practice known as Wabi Sabi. There really are no words in the English language to describe it – as it is more an essence, than something to be described.

Its origins are in ancient Chinese living such as Taoism and Zen Buddhism. Zen priest Murata Shuko of Nara got rid of the gold and fancy tea sets and used rough and wooden instruments. Latre, the famous tea master, Sen no Rikyu of Kyoto constructed a teahouse with a very low door so that even an emperor would have to bow to enter. This was to remind everyone of the importance of humility.

The words to describe Wabi-Sabi are beautiful and remind me of the authenticity of parenting…"the beauty of things that are imperfect, impermanent and incomplete." When we are able to see the beauty in the imperfect, the impermanent and the incomplete, we are able to fully embrace what it means to parent or to teach.

When my children see me cry, break a dish, accidentally swear, mess up my words, have failed relationships, gain weight, lose weight, get angry, be sad over a loss, they get to see the imperfection of my perfectly human self. They get to see that it is o.k. to be and do all of these things. When we parent as if we have all the answers and do not make mistakes it makes us unapproachable to our children and often someone they cannot relate to. We become Superhuman in many ways and our children feel they pale in comparison.

The art of seeing the perfect in the imperfect to me becomes what parenting is all about. The messes, the stops and starts, the turn-arounds, the humility in saying, "I'm sorry" and the gut-wrenching honesty it takes to truly show up to and for your child as your authentic self – warts and all is what Conscious Parenting Strategies is all about. Joining them in their humanity, yet holding your own sense of authority for them to learn from, is a True Connection. It is a precarious balance of leading by example, setting boundaries for security and revealing your True Self that gives you the opportunity to *truly* teach, which is where the word parent originates.

We read books, apply rules and regulations to our parenting. We take classes, consult the Internet, other parents, our doctors and any other number of "experts" on what to do and how to do it. They are all resourceful and necessary. But, when it really comes down to it, WE are the experts. We are the ones who know best what to do. We just have to trust that by living our own authentic truth and being honest with ourselves and our children, the perfection in the "imperfection" will be a true work of heart.

Parenting Through Adolescence
Everything We Do Is To Prepare Us
For This Time

There's a Tiger in the Bathroom

You are probably scratching your head at this point, wondering why talk about teenagers, specifically? What about all the other ages and stages? The sum total of our child's experiences will assimilate into their brain and thus their behavior. It seems a good idea then to discuss what the "end product" will look like before you actually arrive there. Parenting up until about age 10 is relatively "easy" compared to adolescence. This is not a "fear" based comment, just insight into child rearing. Having had five kids in my household, each with their own unique personalities and challenges, I would say that relatively speaking, taking care of a baby, raising a toddler, preschooler and pre-pubescent child has its challenges, but compared to that of a teenager, it's a walk in the park.

When you arrive into "the hood", you are now in the passenger seat of what we now call the Car of your teenager's life, with only a mere emergency (and sometimes faulty) brake between you and a concrete wall. But, not without complete power and control, mind you – we have some resources. But first, let's explore the world of a teenager, shall we.

Have you seen the movie *Hangover*? There's a delightfully hilarious scene where Allan wakes up and goes to the bathroom. He's standing there, completely unaware that there is a tiger in the bathroom. He looks at it, turns back around and there's a good 10 seconds before it actually registers that THERE IS A TIGER IN THE BATHROOM! This is how a lot of parents feel when they wake up one day in their child has hit hormone hell...it takes a little time to register – but you slowly turn around and ask yourself, "WHO is that!? And what have they done with my precious, sweet child!?" From your perspective, as you run screaming from the bathroom, shutting the door, panting and hoping it was just a really bad dream, you realize you are in completely new territory. You are in the "hood" – Teenage-hood...welcome to an altered reality...

The Hood

(The down-low on developmental happenings – straight from the source...your teen...)

Dude, what up? Chill-ax – I'll be in by 12:00 or I'll text you. Look, I totally get that you worry about me. But, if I'm going to learn how to navigate this thing called life, you're gonna have to loosen the noose a little. I mean, if you had never let go of my hand when I was learning to walk, well, you know I'd still be holding your hand which is way not cool. I'll get it – I'll make some mistakes, just cuz well, I haven't figured it all out, yet. But, well – that's what this time is all about, right? Figuring it out.

This is the stage of identity – it's where I take all that I have learned about who YOU think I am, and who the rest of the world thinks I am and decipher – who am I really? I imagine this is an on-going process, but it is the first time I am looking at it closely and questioning it based on what I have internalized about who I am. To do that, it may seem like I'm going out on a ledge...you know – piercings, hair colors, black nail polish, tattoos... It's like play'in dress up "teen style." I have to try some things on to see if they fit me – it's not personal. I'm not diss'in you or your values or any of the things you have taught me. I just need to ask my own questions and get my own answers right now.

Remember, my brain is still growing and changing. My prefrontal cortex, which controls my ability to "think ahead" or identify potential consequences for my actions is not fully developed (it's the control center that sends out signals like "not your best move, dude!"). Yet my limbic system is in high gear – which means my emotions rule over my "thinking self" right now. My brain is listening more to the emotional side of things. My brain is figuring things out by myelination and synaptic pruning. These two processes are making my brain more efficient...but it's seriously still under construction! But, you can help me in this process by providing opportunities for me to build my skills (giving me opportunities to make good choices and

97

live with the consequences - don't keep bail'in me out or making all my decisions for me – not forming any healthy brain connections that way!), to learn (help me pursue my interests outside of school, also), exercise (video games are not a form of exercise...make me move it!) and creative outlets (let me paint, draw, play my drums, guitar....give me something to create).

You help me the most when you just listen. No third degrees or interrogations. When you listen to what I have to say and let me know that it is o.k. to feel what I feel and be who I am, I feel safe and loved. Also, with my emotions all ramped up, when you listen and acknowledge my feelings, it lets me know that I'm not a loser to feel this way. I want to be able to tell you my fears, thoughts and feelings – but only if you promise not to freak out. I will tell someone – the question is, will it be you? I hope so....how you react to my "not so nice emotions and feelings" will determine if you are safe place for me to land. I know I'm not all "pretty" and wrapped up in a bow right now – still totally figuring it out – but I want to know that that's o.k. with you and that you'll hang with me through it all. I don't want you to be my buddy, though – that's totally lame. I need you to be the parent – still setting healthy boundaries for yourself and me. I want you to listen to me like you're 'feel'in me' – you get where I'm coming from. You don't have to agree with me – just listen.

I can't believe I'm saying this, but I really do need to do my own laundry (how will I survive college??) and I should probably know

98

how to make a few meals on my own. Although, I love it when you wake me up in the morning (are you feeling the sarcasm?) – I should probably be on my own in that department – I totally need to regulate my own sleeping habits, for sure. You know research supports me sleep'in in until noon. I know it doesn't necessarily fit into "life" – but, at least it makes sense! My circadian rhythms are completely whacked out! (Bet you didn't even know I knew that huh?)

Yea, having a job stinks sometimes, but it is nice having money and man, life is expensive…glad I'm learning this lesson, now when I'm on your dime! Oh, and I know I grumble about the "household" contribution I must make by way of chores…but, it does make me feel like I am a part of this "family team" – so, I'm really cool with it. I appreciate that you don't ride my butt about it though, like you tell me what needs to be done on Monday and let me take care of it without hassling me. It helps me learn to be responsible – which interestingly enough helps to mature my prefrontal cortex! Whatever!

And while we're do'in the gratitude deal, thanks for not being one of those parents that were always telling me what to do and not letting me make my own choices and live with the consequences when I was younger. I mean, I see kids now who are like totally out of control - it's like they have never been able to figure out life and they're going way crazy. I'm sure their parents didn't set out to send them in this direction – but it all matters, it all adds up. When you allowed me to suffer the consequences of my own bonehead moves without judging me that was cool. I know I didn't seem grateful for that at the time, but I can see where letting me fall a little now and then gave me the opportunity to learn how to stand a little stronger. Oh, and by the way, research totally shows that setting boundaries, living with consequences, appropriate choices and activities that allow me to exercise my autonomy is the way to expedite the process of making connections that help my prefrontal cortex – who knew!?)

And about the "sex talk." I'm so glad you weren't one of those parents that waited until the last minute – like, now – when I totally did NOT want to listen to you about this topic – you know what they say, "Talking to teenagers about sex is like giving a fish a bath!" I'm glad that you gave me little bits and pieces of information all throughout my life. I was able to hear from you when I was curious, asking questions and listening. You gave me the right amount of information by checking in with me. You'd ask me "What do you think about that?" And then you would expand on what I understood or correct me when I was totally way off (remember when I thought you had a baby by eating baby seeds because Grandpa told me that the pregnant woman I saw had eaten too many watermelon seeds and now there was a watermelon growing in her belly! I didn't eat watermelons that whole summer!) It allowed me to form a good foundation so that when my friends are talking about it, I can filter it through that. I get it. You didn't preach your values to me. You lived them, I was watching.

Oh, and one last thing – my grades. Thanks for handing over the responsibility for my grades, well, to me. I know I don't always handle that so well – but I am learning that it really is all about me. If I fail, I have to learn how to pick myself up and move on. I know you worry about college and me getting into one. But, I guess that will be my problem too. If I don't own the problem, I guess I can't fix it. And sure, it'd be great to have you "fix" it – but you can't really do that. Only I can. So, I'm glad you have transferred the responsibility for my grades to me...now, I'll just have to do something with it....bummer. But, your gentle, clever reminders don't fall on deaf ears. I am listening even when I'm pretending not to. I like it when you turn the responsibility back to me. I may bulk at it, but ultimately it lets me know you believe in me and my ability to figure it out. That rocks! And yes, I do love it when you tell me, but more when you show me you love me. I still like hugs and need them. But, I won't necessarily ask for them. – Peace out.

When we are parenting consciously, we are employing strategies that are continually pointing our child back to themselves. We want them to have the ability to think for themselves and to make decisions and understand what the natural consequences of their decision look like. As we continue to do this, when they become adolescents, they can think for themselves, make appropriate decisions and balance a very actively engaged amygdala (gas) with a healthy prefrontal cortex (brake).

I emphasize this a lot as I see too many parents in my office who were the 'brake" for their kids until adolescents and now it is very difficult because the teen is all "gas". This is difficult to rectify. It is not impossible but a lot of power struggles need to be let go of.

This is a small snapshot of adolescents just as an "end-game" perspective. We are slowly, intentionally and consciously transferring the responsibility over to our children so that when they get here, they are prepared.

Teaching About Cell Phone Usage

I think I would be remiss in talking about teenagers without a cursory look at teens and their cell phones. With the rampant use of cell phones these days many kids are not given parameters. You might add to these guidelines, and/or look at having a contract with your child (I have a free downloadable file on my website: http://www.monsterproofyourchild.com/downloads/sample-cell-phone-contract/. But I think having a "say" about cell phone usage (especially until there are more studies that show us the results of long-term usage) when a phone is first handed to a child is a good idea.

- Turn it off at night. Have a time every night that the phone gets cradled and your child "unplugs". So many kids sleep with their phones by their heads. This is not good for their growing and developing brains and they are on high alert all night.

- No sending of nude pictures. Ever. If they receive a nude picture, they need to tell an adult.

- Teach them to finish their phone conversation before getting in line to check out.

- Teach them that if they are having a personal and private conversation, do not have it in a public place.

- No sending threatening messages or using the phone to "bully".

103

- Have them know and understand your plan (how many minutes they have and what your expectations are for their usage).

- They are responsible for taking care of their phone, keeping it charged and following the rules at school regarding usage.

Chapter 3 Brain (& Mind) Development

We want to mostly focus on the mind in this section. But, we must look at a basic understanding of the brain, how it develops and functions as a whole in order to understand how the mind works. The best description of the difference between the brain and the mind I have heard is that the brain is the physical place that the mind resides in.

The brain is the only organ not fully formed at birth. A baby is born with 100 billion brain cells. The brain is only 25% of its full size. By age two, 80% of the brain is intact (that is a lot, a lot of brain connections being made within the first two years of life!) All of this work takes two times the amount of energy used by an adult (which explains why our children need more sleep but also more patience...they are doing a whole lot of construction right now!) By age six, it is 90% of its adult size. It has 1,000 trillion synapses (or connections). But by age 10, half of these die through a process called "pruning" which is necessary to make our systems more efficient.[15]

But a brain grows by stimulation. If the right amount of stimulation at the right time does not occur, a slowdown in a very important area can occur. Researches at Baylor college of Medicine show that children who do not play or who are not touched have brains that are 20-30% smaller than normal (which supports the importance of play in the previous chapter!). [16] But the process of development is one that cannot, nor should it be rushed. The concept "at the right time" is important. Often, we look at ages as an indication of the "right time" but we must look at the development of the brain, how it typically develops, but also what happens when there are interruptions to this development and how that impedes or slows down subsequent factors in development. Unfortunately, it is not always apparent or obvious.

What follows is an overview of the developing brain, which aides in the understanding of why children behave the way they do from a brain-based perspective.

Dr. Paul McLean outlined a "triune brain", one in which there are three distinct "brains":

The Reptilian brain – which is instinctive behavior- brain

The Mammalian brain – which is the emotional   brain

The Neocortex brain – which is the thinking brain

When we are dealing with our children, it is important to ascertain from which "brain" they operating from and respond with the appropriate action.

Seriously simplifying this, the brain develops in three stages: The Brainstem, which correlates to the Reptilian brain, The Midbrain, which correlates to the Mammalian Brain and The Cortex, which correlates to The Human (Neocortex) Brain.

Here is a brief description of each:

The Reptilian Brain

The reptilian brain or R-complex as it is often referred to is involved in our actual physical survival and maintenance of the body. The characteristics of the Reptilian brain are that they are ritualistic in nature, automatic and incredibly resistant to change. When the reptilian brain is in use there is an animalistic and instinctive behavior that is going on which is not based on any logic, and when the child is in this mode, all messages to higher level thinking are blocked. Temper tantrums are indicative of reptilian brain and can happen at any age. Not getting a toy at Target does not seem to us to be a logical reason to have a melt-down. But, when your child, with their limited feedback loops to the cortex, which enhance brain function, interprets the situation from their reptilian brain, there is no logic involved, so reasoning and explaining will fall on deaf ears. What is necessary in this situation is action – no words, or minimal at that.

Neurotransmitter imbalances can throw anyone back into the Reptilian brain state. For example, cravings (chocolate!)

A pre-emptive strike for temper tantrums lies within us. The reptilian brain creates a heightened state of awareness and our little ones smell fear and frustration instinctually and will feed off of this. Here is an exercise you can do with incredible effectiveness from 3-10 minutes a day. You will probably find its benefits so far-reaching that you will do it several times a day. Find a calming c.d. – music that is light and beautiful. Burn a few copies so that you have a c.d. in your car, kitchen, on your iPod, etc. For practice, find a quiet moment (I am aware that this might only be somewhere between the hours of midnight and 4:00 A.M. – but find a few moments for yourself). Put the music on and begin this simple breathing exercise.

Imagine an imaginary ball going up the little hill (breathe long, slow breaths in through your nose), at the top of the hill, hold for a moment, then as the imaginary ball goes down the hill, breathe long slow breaths out your mouth. While you are doing this, think of a thought that creates a warm, loving feeling in the middle of your chest. We are looking at opening up our heart chakra – usually, for me a thought of holding my child for the first time, or a sweet moment with them will create this type of feeling. But, find whatever works for you. Repeat with the music for 3-10 minutes. Try to do this for at least three minutes 2X a day. Use the same music each time. What we are doing is based on B.F. Skinners "conditioned response." We are going to teach our body to calm down when it hears this music. When you are in a heightened state of arousal (techno talk for at your wit's end!), put on the music and create this state of calm. Eventually, you will "hear" this in your head and it can trigger the relaxing breath automatically.

It is a practice and re-training of the breath. You can train your child in the same way. Obviously, during a meltdown is not the time to do this training. But, when we train during the calm, when the storm hits, we have a safe respite that is only a breath away. There are many phone apps for this as well. Currently, I use My Calm Beat (it's a great thing to "train" your child a slowing down their breath during calm moments and then utilize it to "remind" them and bring them back to calm during the not-so-calm moments!)

The major point about this lower-level "thinking" brain is it is very primitive. When our child's basic needs are not met, they block all other signals from this part of the brain to higher parts (as in "thinking" is out the window!). Utilizing some CPS strategies (Stop, Drop and Roll) are helpful because we get low (in stature and voice) and use minimal language (which requires minimal processing). We make sure the child is safe, provide unconditional love, which "calms" this reptilian brain, maintain boundaries ("Feet on floor"), and allow for choices, when appropriate.

The Mammalian Brain

The Mammalian brain is the emotional brain and is connected to the limbic system. It correlates to memory, attention and motivation. It can facilitate learning or it can block thinking altogether. It creates loops with the lower and higher centers (reptilian and thinking brain). It houses the amygdala, which serves as a filter for incoming

111

experiences through our fears and past experience. It attaches a sort of emotional "tickler file" system so that we can classify experiences (is this harmful for me?) One can have an experience as a child that can imprint here and create a negative connection and logic is of no value. For example, when my son was 3 ½ we went to a friend's house and their little dog jumped up on him and he fell over and the dog was playing and licking him, but in those few moments before I could get him, it was an incredibly powerful negative experience. Even though he has completely recovered from autism, he still does not like dogs.

The Mammalian brain also houses the hippocampus, which is involved in memory storage and also helps us to filter what we actual retain. The functioning of the hippocampus can be reduced by chronic stress. In order to learn, a balance must be created that is challenging, but not negatively emotionally charged. Play becomes an important part of learning in this regard for it offers opportunities to try things out. We also know that fear-based tactics inhibit learning in this area of the brain. [17]

The Neocortex

The Neocortex, cerebral cortex or "thinking brain" makes up five-sixths of the entire brain. It facilities language - including speech and writing. In addition, it is responsible for logical and formal operational thinking and allows us to think and plan for the future. It has two regions, one for processing sensory information and the other for voluntary movement.

Three Brains In One

It has been suggested that these three brains are interconnected, however to what extent is not known. Although it is not known whether they work independently or not, it is proposed that at one time or another one particular brain may be dominant over the others. In addition, these three brains can be viewed as the mind, body and spirit: the mind, being the neocortex, the body, the reptilian brain and the spirit the mammalian brain.

So from a brain-based perspective the integration of mind, body and spirit creates a "whole brain" and the fluid interconnectedness of these three brains is what allows a human being to be whole: a thinking, feeling, and behaving "being." What is optimal is the manifestation of the highest consciousness in each one of these brains.

The most important thing to keep in mind from all of this is that at any moment, our child can be operating from one healthy, integrated brain or (more likely, in particular during stages of major development) they are reverting back to one of the "lower brain" levels. When we are aware of this, we can parent more effectively and direct the learning of the child more appropriately.

Young children must involve their bodies to learn. The motor cortex is the first area to mature in both hemispheres, which is the first way in which young children organize their brains. Involving as many senses as possible helps to create a strong inner-communication system within the brain. This helps a child learn to look at the details, evaluate them, organize them and then make plans for the future. One way in which a child can expand their intelligence is through arts. This allows nontraditional learners (or learners with different learning styles) another way to learn.

One incredibly powerful way that children organize their brains is through big motor movement. Movement is integral (rocking, playing, hanging from the monkey bars) in the development of the cerebellum or what we used to call "play".

What we want more than anything is to teach our children to think, learn and explore – new thoughts. Not, just regurgitate the old ones. In reviewing how the brain works, it's important to have an overview of understanding, but the main objective and goal is to continually ask ourselves how we can instill in our child a passion for learning, questioning and discovering, for themselves. We want to awaken and nurture within them their innate sense of curiosity, need to explore and discover the meaning in all things.

So, how do children learn?

Albert Bandura theorized that we all learn through modeled behavior. It has been shown that children learn through imitation. There are four factors that are necessary for learning to occur: **Attention** (we have to be paying attention, although often times children pick up on things that we do not *think* they are paying attention to…we all know those words that pick up and use at precisely the wrong time and we did not think they heard us!) **Remembering** what it is we were paying attention to (this has a lot to do with how much of an impact this actually made on us…was it memorable and was it attached to a good, strong emotion?) **Reproduction** (can we repeat what we learned and are we capable of doing that and have the right physical abilities?) For instance, the mouth cannot produce what the ear does not hear, so children who have auditory processing difficulties or have auditory problems might not be able to produce certain sounds. Lastly, is **Motivation** (a good reason to repeat the behavior).[18]

The Power of Thoughts and Intentions

Now that we have a basic understanding of how the brain works and how children learn, we move into the area of the mind and our thoughts. There is a lot of new information and data supporting the power of our thoughts and intentions. One book, *The Intention Experiment* by Lynne McTaggart looks at a host of scientific data regarding the power of thought and intention. Scientific evidence points to the fact that thoughts are able to affect finished, solid matter. In other words, we have the power with our thoughts and intentions to affect everything! This is no longer just an idea, it is based on scientific data! Experiment after experiment conclusively shows that not only are we receivers of signals of energy, but we are also transmitters. This sounds more like science fiction than science, but if you stop to think about it, you have experienced the energy that someone is emitting that makes you feel good or bad. It does not seem that far-fetched of an idea when you look at it in a practical way.

One experiment involved healers who sent an intention to affect the molecular structure of water. When examined under a microscope, there *were* significant changes in the structure of the water. This was all achieved through intention. The interesting result is that the control group, who were not healers, did not have the same effect. The master healers had the most significant effect, which demonstrates that intention is a skill that some are better at than others.

A study looking at master mediators (monks) had the highest levels of gamma activity, which produces permanent emotional improvement because it activates the left anterior portion of the brain, which is associated with joy. They were literally attuned to happiness all of the time. Although most of us will never achieve this level of mastery, it would stand to reason that a little bit of achievement in this area, starting at a young age, nurtured over a long period of time could produce a level of competency that could produce amazing results. The worst that would happen would be feeling happy some of the time. The best case would be feeling happy all of the time. Seems like a "no brainer" to me (sorry, I couldn't resist!)

With the rampant diagnosis of Attention Deficit Disorder and Attention Deficit Hyperactivity Disorder (ADD/ADHD), the lack of attention of young people gets a lot of attention (pun intended). Concentrated focus, which is achieved in meditation, creates an integration of the left and right hemispheres of the brain, creating a harmonious communication. Sara Lazar is a neuroscientist at Massachusetts General Hospital and expert in functional magnetic resonance imaging (fMRI). She was enlisted by Herbert Benson to study meditators who meditated for 20-60 minutes per day. They discovered that the areas in the brain that were associated with sensory processing and awareness and attention were thicker in the mediators than in the controls. This research shows some of the first evidence that meditation causes permanent changes in the brain. [19]

Other research conducted demonstrates that the thought of an action (in the case of athletes performing) can create the same neuro-transmission as performing the action itself! That is why most athletes speak to how so much of their game is "mental." An experiment where individuals 20-35 years old were asked to imagine flexing one of their biceps as hard as they could 5 times a week. There was a 13.5 increase in muscle size in just a few weeks (with NO physical exertion at all!).[20]

Everyone has heard of the placebo affect, as well, where someone is given a pseudo treatment (sugar pill, for example) and told it is a medication that could cure whatever ails them. It has repeatedly been shown that this is incredibly effective!

The most powerful evidence of intention and thoughts are of visualizations where we "see" the event that we want yet engage our senses in a way that it is perceived as if it were happening in the present. One example of this is to do a daily dry run each morning. Having your child "view" the day the way he or she wants it to go as if it is going to go that way. This is incredibly powerful!

The most disturbing information from these experiments is the power of negative thoughts. Experiments that involved negative thoughts produced disturbing results in that negative thoughts produced greater results than positive thoughts. It is another precaution to guard our thoughts carefully.

In 1985, a group of Tibetan Buddhist monks sat quietly in meditation. They were scantily clad, sitting high in the Himalayas in northern India with temperatures approaching freezing. Instead of any appearance of being cold, the monks began to sweat. They were covered with new sheets, drenched in cold water, which quickly dried. Scientists studied these monks and this extraordinary phenomenon, where they had lowered their metabolism by 60% ("experienced mediators" can decrease metabolism by 17%). Through the power of thought ONLY, they had literally used their bodies to boil freezing water! These are masters of intention, for sure, but it speaks to the power of our thoughts over even extreme conditions. [21]

So, what does any of this have to do with your child's developing mind? THOUGHTS create our realities…our intentions are who we become. What WE intend and think for our children becomes a sort of entrainment, where they connect with what it is we are holding in our intention for who they are. We teach our children about the power of our intentions and our thoughts by how we live and what we demonstrate to them through our words and our deeds. If we (the parents), family, friends, are not holding a collective thought and intention of our child's highest good and potential, who will? If the teachers, school, principals, therapist and US are all determined to see what is "wrong" with our child and not what is "good" (even when it is not clearly evident), how do we possibly hope to excavate it?

It is our role to hold a "space" and an intention for them to grow. To believe in their innate Divinity and reflect it back to them when there little lights go dim.

Memes and Our Children's Thoughts

Richard Brodie wrote *Virus of the Mind* and the science of memetics is explored. Memetics is the study of memes. A meme becomes anything that gets imitated. Remember what scientests and developmental specialists say about how children learn? By imitation. Our children our absorbing memes at a record rate considering all of the information they have available through mutli-mediums at this point. If you do not think you are affected by a meme, think of Coke (which is now synonomous with cola – when in fact, it is a BRAND), or Kleenex…(that's a brand name – not "facial tissue."). Also, think of the "low fat" diets that most everyone went on. Or now how everyone is looking for products labeled "whole grain" (when in fact a lot of them are not.). Think of the muffins they serve at Starbucks? You would probaby not eat a 600 calorie piece of cake for breakfast, but if it is called a muffin, you might consider it. If you have ever participated in a chain letter, that's a meme. Now, some memes are good…when you see a person crossing in a crosswalk, you stop. When you see a cop, you slow down.

Richard Brodie points out that memes do not have to be truthful to perpetuate. But, ideas that make sense will replicate more quickly than those that do not. Religions that have answered all of the tough questions are easier for people than religions that require one to ask the tough questions and seek answers. The answers do not have to be truthful, they just have to be easy to understand.

Our attraction to memes is rooted in our reptilian brain. It is the part of our brain that is based on survival and is "juiced up" by fear. Granted, there are very few things in our lives that threaten our very survival during this day and age, yet we are still programmed to be afraid.

What scientists have discovered is that our thoughts are not always our own original ideas. We can actually "catch" a thought like a virus. We spread these "viruses" simply by communicating and we are knee-deep in communication in this day and age. You can "catch" a mind virus simply by reading the newspaper or reading the headlines on the Internet. There have been many viruses spread via the Internet that have turned out *not* to be true, but many people believe them, anyway. The real problem with mind viruses is that each time we take on a new one, we add more stress to our lives. This might be o.k. for us as adults, but our children are being inundated with mind viruses and it can cause unnecessary stress.

What is the most concerning is not so much the memes that are "out there" but the ones that are being absorbed at home, even without our awareness. How many kids feel inadequate or "stupid" even though they might not ever be told that, but there is an underlying feeling of unworthiness that is fostered. We know how powerful our intentions and are thoughts are. Our kids are absorbing this. If a child grows up with a feeling of inadequacy or feeling stupid, it is part of their belief system and that is very hard to change. Remember, our children live from ages 2-6 in a highly suggestible and programmable state. At this age, children are so highly influential and they are learning through imitation. So, although you may be telling them one thing, they are watching and imitating what you say and do. Children are incredibly intuitive at this stage, too and pick up on things that are not said, as well.

If we are going to rectify the false memes of our children, we have to question our own belief systems and then go about re-conditioning *ourselves*. Then, we move onto our children. For example, if your fundamental belief is there is not enough (love, time, money, opportunities, etc.) in the world, you will perpetuate that "meme" for yourself and for your child. Most likely, this was not your original thought, but a belief system that you were infected with during your influential years. However, we cannot change what we are not aware of. So, we need to examine our fundamental beliefs and our children can often "bring them up" for us to review. If we do this honestly and compassionately we can truly "disinfect" this virus and heal...way down deep - a gift for ourselves, and our child!

One way we can "re-think" this is to question the belief. So, if we believe there is a lack, we ask if it is really true and then we must re-condition ourselves to "see" and believe in abundance. If our child is infected with the "I am stupid" virus, we need to find immunizing ways to disinfect. We do this by affirming their abilities when we see them doing something that would indicate otherwise.

Another way our brains are infected is something called cognitive dissonance. If our minds cannot make sense of something, it will struggle until it can somehow reconcile it. So, when we try to disinfect with a new thought, our brain is running around in circles going, "I don't know what to do here...I don't know what to do here..." We have to create some harmony or a bridge, so in the lack situation, "Although it appears as though there is not enough, it is simply a temporary state. I have enough, there is enough, I create abundance." With our child and their "I am stupid" meme, we help them bridge this. We do this by employing our CPS skills of actively listening, but then we must serve as a bridge until they are able to do this themselves. "Getting an "F" on a test does not make you stupid. It means you did not know the material. I remember when you got a 100% on a spelling test. That means you knew the words. Your ability to figure out how to learn the material in one situation can transfer to another situation. This is what makes you smart."

What we are continually doing is trying to find out where our child is at with their meme, where they would be if they thought a new thought and facilitate a bridge between the two until they are able to do this themselves. As we model it in our own lives (as in talking through our own cognitive dissonance so our children can hear our process as well), they "pick up" on and will model this behavior. "I don't have any money. Wait. Let's look at this, I do have money, I just used it to pay all of my bills right now. More money will come in and right now, my bills are paid, I have food, we have a home, I have a car and look, we all have clothes on!"

One other thought about our children's minds is that we must review what they see and put into their minds. Our children have access to so much information and images that they might not be developmentally prepared for. Research states that when children watch scary moves, their limbic system (which is their emotional center) lights up as if they were under threat. [22] It is important to guard our children's minds, as what they think about, they become.

In today's society, it is no longer enough to teach our children what to think. They must be given the tools to think for themselves. But, learning how to think (and the true power of thoughts) is a process and it starts at home, with us. When we understand how the brain functions, how our child learns, the power of thoughts and intentions, we parent consciously and "mind" our P's & Q's. ☺

Chapter 4   Nourishing the Body of a Child

The point of this section is to ensure that your child's body facilitates the growth of their entire being – mind, body and spirit. This section looks at basic nutrition only. A diet rich in nutrients and nourishing foods will facilitate this. Read labels. Our children are getting a lot more in their food than we did and most of it is not good for them. We have to get very clever about finding healthy foods to replace the oh-so-attractive-packaged-foods being passed off as "food" in the lunchroom. Always consult your doctor, a nutritionist and other expert advice when dealing with challenging health issues. The more "experts" one consults, the better in order to get a well-rounded view. But here are some basic guidelines are as follows:

Things to avoid:

- Genetically modified foods (look for organic or Non-GMO Project seals).

- Artificial colors, sweeteners and preservatives.

- Excessive sugar.

- Excessive fruit juices (high in sugar).

- Energy drinks (or caffeine).

- Excessive video games & Internet (on/off electronics).

- Excessive chemicals in the shampoo, soaps and lotions our children use (look for natural products).

Check for:

- Allergies or heavy metal toxicity.

- Hidden stresses (learning difficulties or possible processing disorders can often go undiagnosed).

Include:

- Plenty of exercise (lots of aerobic activity).

- Thymus Thump (which is a gentle "knocking' on the middle of the chest with a closed fist for about 20 seconds while smiling, breathing deeply in and out and saying "ha, ha, ha". (This exercise can neutralize negative thoughts and creates a sense of peace and general well-being).

- Have child cross arms over chest, grab opposite ear lobes with hands and just bend at the knees and go up and down 3 times).

- Deep breathing/relaxation exercises.

- Meditation.

- Balanced diet for the growing brain - protein diet/whole grains/complex carbohydrates

- Fats (Olive oil, avocados, nuts, fish oils).

- Plenty of water.

- Look at supplements: Good Multivitamin & Fish oils (research shows that the ADHD brain is deficient in essential fatty acids0.

- Plenty of sleep (routines are very important).

- To help ground your child (or help them feel more in their bodies), provide a "deep tissue" massage. Start with the child's dominant hand and provide firm pressure – a nice "squeeze" kind of hug going all the way up the hand and arm and continue with other arm and then both legs. Spending about 30 seconds on each limb. This feels nice and helps "ground" the child back into their body – especially if they are out-of-control. You can do a gentle head massage as well.

- As children get older, make them aware of how food makes them feel. Encourage them to keep a food journal and list how certain foods make them feel. The more we teach our children about energy and how to pay attention to their bodies, the more we empower them.

> ### *Extra help for children who struggle with attention:*

- Have child write things down.

- Check for understanding (have them repeat back to you what you said).

- Keep a visual schedule.

- Make sure they are "belly breathing" and breathing through their nose.

- Have them do a cross pattern march before sitting down to "learn" (this is where they march around the room and cross over their body and hit the left knee with the right palm and right knee with the left palm, while marching).

- Practice saying random numbers or objects in groups of 5, 6, or 7 to increase your child's auditory processing. For example, say, "1-5-6-7-8" and have them repeat it back to you. You want to say this monotone, and equally spaced apart. You'll continue giving random sequences of numbers (move down to a 4 digit number sequence, if 5 is too difficult and then move back up). Most children should be able to do about a 7-digit sequence. If your child is struggling, just keep working with it. Even one increase (going from a 4 digit span to a 5 digit span) will make a huge difference in their ability to retain information.

Other recommendations:

- Rainbows and Sunshine (AGES 6 to 11): relaxation mind-body CD developed with pediatricians to help children relax, sleep, and heal at home and in hospitals. Recommended for insomnia, stress, anxiety, IBS, injuries, phobias, ADD/ ADHD, surgery, cancer... [Single] (Can be found at Amazon.com).

- Also you can search on YouTube for meditations for kids. There are many very good ones on there.

- Dr. Daniel Amen's "Healing ADD" book.

- Games that increase focus/attention & memory: "Memory", Chinese Checkers, Chess, CLUE, Simon, BOP It!

Chakras

We are pure energy and it is helpful to understand our bodies (what makes us feel good would be energy supporting and what makes us feel bad would be energy depleting). Our bodies have energy centers known as chakras. Understanding the 7 energy centers (chakras) help us to aid our children in their bodies as well. Knowing what each particular energy center is relating to is helpful as well.

- The First Chakra is the Root chakra, located at the base of the spine. The color associated with it is red. It is our grounding charka and the physical need is safety and behavior shows up as fear. Imbalance shows up as anxiety. A calming smell (cinnamon) will help balance this chakra or the sound "O" (long sound) or providing protein.

- The Second Chakra is the Sacral chakra, located below the navel. The color associated with it is orange. It is the relationship & emotions chakra and the need for closeness or letting things go and behavior shows up as constant wanting. Imbalance shows up as a cold. Drinking water and the sound "ooh" provides balance for this chakra.

- The Third Chakra is the Navel chakra, located at the solar plexus. The color associated with it is yellow. It is the center of will power and the issue is Self Control. Imbalance shows up as anger. It can affect areas in our stomach. Whole grains and the sound "ah" can help balance this chakra.

134

- The Fourth Chakra is the Heart chakra, located in the heart area. The color associated with it is green. It is the chakra of balance, love and connection. Imbalance shows up in areas of trust and love. Rose incense, the sound "A" (long sound) and eating vegetables balance this chakra.

- The Fifth Chakra is the Throat chakra, located at the neck (throat). The color associated with it is blue. It is the energy center for communication and healing and imbalance shows up with the inability to speak truth or in unclear expression. Eucalyptus is a balancing smell, fruit and the sound "Ee" are also good balancing tools for this chakra.

- The Sixth Chakra is the Third Eye chakra, located between the physical eyes. The color associated with it is indigo. It is the center of intuition and understanding. We nurture this energy center with lavender, "Mmm" sounds and great breathing techniques.

- The Seventh Chakra is the Crown chakra and located at the top of the head. The color associated with it is violet and it is our center of spiritual understanding and connectedness. The scent Jasmine and the sound "Ng" are associated with opening this chakra.

Just creating greater awareness for our children about the fact that they are energy and that everything is energy is so helpful. They can "pay attention" to how things make them feel. You can also use "applied kinesiology" with your children. This is where you have your child hold something over their heart (start with an apple, for example) with the right hand and hold their left arm straight out with a gentle fist at the end. You will tell them to close their eyes and with the apple over their heart, you will try to push their arm down with two fingers. When something makes us "strong" the child is able to hold the arm up with no difficulties. If something makes us "weak", we cannot (despite all our best efforts) hold our arm up.

This is fun and the kids will try and try to make those Oreos keep their arms up! It is fun to do this with music, or even "thoughts" or put random things in bags so that you don't know what they are. It is a playful way of educating your child about energy and how things affect our bodies.

Also, get the book, "The Hidden Messages In Water" by Masaru Emoto. It's interesting to look at and talk about how our thoughts can affect water. Kids really love these "real life" (and scientific) approaches to the spiritual concepts we are planting. It gives the left-brain something to do, too!

Chapter 5 Nourishing the Innate Spirit of a Child

There was once a small boy who banged a drum all day and loved every moment of it. He would not be quiet, no matter what anyone else said or did. Various people who called themselves Sufis, and other well-wishers, were called in by neighbors and asked to do something about the child. The first so-called Sufi told the boy that he would, if he continued to make so much noise, perforate his eardrums; this reasoning was too advanced for the child, who was neither a scientist nor a scholar. The second told him that drum beating was a sacred activity and should be carried out only on special occasions. The third offered the neighbors plugs for their ears; the fourth gave the boy a book; the fifth gave the neighbors books that described a method of controlling anger through biofeedback; the sixth gave the boy meditation exercises to make him placid and explained that all reality was imagination. Like all placebos, each of these remedies worked for a short while, but none worked for very long.

Eventually, a real Sufi came along. He looked at the situation, handed the boy a hammer and chisel, and said, "I wonder what is INSIDE the drum?"

This chapter is last because all that we do is an opportunity to engage our child's innate spirit. They live in this space and when we invite them to explore what's "inside" it all, they are intrigued and willing and playful participants. They will often lead us into places we ourselves were uncertain existed.

We teach them techniques of breathing, lighting a candle (battery operated, of course!), providing meditation cards, sample prayers, fun crystals and soft music and we offer them tools for calming themselves down.

But, mostly we continually mirror back to them their innate wonder and their Divine Perfection! All of the ways in which we tend to their bodies and teach them to do so, and clear their minds and ways in which we parent are all for the sacred purpose of connecting them with their Inner Light. We are here to help them find out what their purpose is and how they best get to express the music that plays within their soul and only theirs.

We do this in the way we play. We do this in the way we honor and respect their individual needs. We do this by setting healthy boundaries (for them and for us). We do this by honoring our own path and commitment to a spiritual practice that resonates with us and keeps us connected to our Divine Source. We do this in how we eat, how we treat grumpy clerks at the store, how we help a friend in need, give to the homeless shelters, volunteer our time, share our resources, and speak about others when they are not around.

How we treat our children when they are weak, down on their luck, broken, tired, sad, angry, when they are vulnerable in front of us, how we show up for them is what they learn as the "face of God". In our eyes, they see Divine Love being conscious of Itself through us.

All Spiritual Experiences are Unique

When asked to explain their spiritual experience, people used over 5500 words and no common terminology was ascertained. This points to how each spiritual experience is highly individualized. We do not know what it is our child has come here to learn. But we do know that a connection to their Divine Nature not only nourishes their spirit, it actually changes their brain.[23]

There is research that states when we contemplate God enough, our neural functioning begins to change. In other words, when we think of God, God becomes "neurologically real". If one sees God as benevolent and providing a sense of comfort and security then God enhances your life. However, if one sees God as vindictive, it can actually "damage" your brain. Long-term contemplation of God and other spiritual values will permanently alter the parts of our brains that control our moods and help shape our sensory perception of the world.

Meditative and contemplative practices strengthen a neurological circuit that promotes peacefulness, compassion for others and social awareness. Spiritual practices can be used to help with greater creativity, communication and understanding.

Study of nuns and Buddhists, found decreased activity in the parietal lobe. When this happens, one's sense of self begins to dissolve, this is a feeling of being "in the flow" or the "zone". This increases one's ability to reach his or her goals.

Meditation and contemplation of God, not only soothes the soul, it changes our brains and our physiology. It is an important component in helping our children "tame the monster-thoughts".

There are several meditations we can do with our child. We can teach them to count their breaths. We can have them breathe in for 4, hold for 7 and release for 8. We can have them do this a few times.

We can take a prayer and have them picture the words on a "blackboard" in their minds. For instance, the prayer of protection, "The Light of God surrounds me." Have them picture the words "the" and "light". Have them place their attention to the "blank" space in between the two words and breathe. Then, they go onto the next two words, and so forth.

You can do a "Mind Adventure". This is where you go on an adventure, in your mind. My daughter and I take "rainbow swings" and slide down on rainbows and go to grandmother tree, where we put all the concerns we have in the basket outside the tree. Then we sit under the tree and "listen" to see if there is a message. Let your child expand this – make it rich. Boys like more active adventures. Do an "add-a-story" component, where you begin telling a story and have them finish it "in their dreams" and discuss it in the morning. If you are not feeling very creative, start reading a story and then change the ending or have your child add to the story.

Another beautiful way to meditate is with an affirmation. Make cards (take index cards and write simple affirmations and hole punch them and connect them with a key ring). Have simple affirmations: I am a genius. I am loved. I am healthy. I am abundant. I am one with God. I am whole and perfect. Anything with an "I Am" is an affirmation to the Universe about what we want. Your child can sit with a battery candle and hold their cards and repeat the affirmation. Even if they do this for 30 seconds before bedtime, we are "planting" a seed of awareness and allowing it to grow.

Have them come up with a meditation and lead you in it. They love this! You will be surprised at the "ritual" they can come up with. My daughter and I do full moon celebrations. We take mini-vanilla wafers (moon cakes of course!) and have a tea party outside on the trampoline under the full moon. She organized our last ritual in which we wrote down things we wanted to bring in, with the full moon on rocks and we left them out under the moon. We have also written things we wanted to "release" on sticks and walked into the desert and released them. The possibilities are endless!

Connecting with our child's innate spiritual self is easy. If we drop into the essence of who we are (because our child already lives in this space!), we become willing playmates. We roll around where our Wonderchild still lives, open our hearts wide with the intention of connecting and loving unconditionally, we parent consciously and everything flows freely from this place.

The "Monster" is shushed in all of us and we play through life with reckless abandon!

One day a student went to his teacher for help.

"What am I doing wrong, Master? I plant seeds in

my garden but they never come up."

"Tell me exactly what you're doing,"

Said the Teacher.

"Well, every day I plant and water. Then at night, I

go to sleep, but in the middle of the night, I wake up

and get worried that the seeds might not be growing.

So, I go outside, dig them up and sure enough,

they're not growing!"

"Hmm...I think I understand your problem,"

Said the Teacher.

About the Author

Dr. Lisa Smith was born and raised in Ohio but moved to Phoenix, AZ twenty-three years ago where she currently resides with 4 of her 5 children. When Lisa's son was diagnosed with autism at age 3 ½ she began a passionate quest comprised of research, education and hands-on experience and she created a program that ultimately led to the remediation of her son's autism. Now, at age 21, he is considered indistinguishable from his peers! She has taken this life-learning, coupled with a Master's Degree in Child and Adolescent Developmental Psychology, a Master's and Doctorate in Metaphysics and Transpersonal Counseling, certification in Family Effectiveness Training, and as a Neurodevelopmentalist to assist other families. Her life mission is to share this eclectic experience and knowledge to help parents to parent consciously or "on purpose". She works with families of all kinds to create a business model for parenting with a program known as ESP (Effective Strategies for Parenting) and teaches CPS (Conscious Parenting Strategies) for effective parenting. Lisa believes that all behavior is a language and teaches parents to interpret this language. She also believes that effective strategies must incorporate the child's mind, body and spirit to create strong efficacy and self-esteem. These integrated practices create a whole child who is "monster-proof" for life!

Lisa hosts workshops around the country, has authored six books and is available for private consultation.

Other Books by Dr. Lisa M. Smith

Do Not, I Say DO NOT Think of a Pink Elephant

Mommy, What Does Love Look Like?

My Brother has Oddism: A Child's Misinterpretation of the Diagnosis of Autism

Dear Kenton Can You Hear Me? Love Mommy

The Tao of Parenting:The Path to Peaceful Parenting

Notes

[1] Milteer, R., Ginsburg, K., 2011. *The Importance of Play In Promoting Healthy Child Development and Maintaining Strong Parent-Child Bond: Focus on Children in Poverty,* 2011. Elk Grove Village, IL: Council on Communications and Media Committee on Psychosocial Aspects of Child and Family Health.

[2] Hofferth, S.L. 1999. *Changes in American Children's Time,* 1981-1997. Ann Arbor: University of Michigan Press.

[3] Milteer, R., Ginsburg, K., 2011. *The Importance of Play In Promoting Healthy Child Development and Maintaining Strong Parent-Child Bond: Focus on Children in Poverty,* 2011. Elk Grove Village, IL: Council on Communications and Media Committee on Psychosocial Aspects of Child and Family Health.

[4] Brown, S., 2009. *Play.* NY: Avery.

[5] Donaldson, O. 1993. *Playing By Heart,* Deerfield Beach, FL: Health Communications, Inc.

[6] Donaldson, O. 1993. *Playing By Heart,* Deerfield Beach, FL: Health Communications, Inc.

[7] brainwave frequency of children

[8] Cohen, L., 2012. *Playful Parenting,* NY: Ballantine Books

[9] Cohen, L., 2012. *Playful Parenting,* NY: Ballantine Books.

[10] Nielsen's 2012 Social Media Report. 2012. www.frankwbaker.com/mediause.htm

[11] kids and technology

[12] Ginott, H., 1965. *Between Parent and Child,* NY: Three Rivers Press.

[13] Mischel, W., Shoda, Y., Rodriguez, M. 1989. Delay of Gratification in Children: *Science* (244) 933-938.

[14] Badenoch, B. 2008. *Being A Brain-Wise Therapist,* NY: W.W. Norton & Company.

[15] Healy, J. 2004. *Your Child's Growing Mind: Brain Development and Learning From Birth to Adolescence,* NY: Three Rivers Press.

[16] Brown, S. 2010. *Play,* NY: Penguin.

[17] Wiltgen, B., Sanders, M., Anagnostaras, S., Sage, J., Fanselow, M. 2012. *Context Fear Leaning in the Absence of the Hippocampus*, Journal of Neuroscience, 26(20).

[18] Bandura, A. (1997). *Self-efficacy: The exercise of control*. NY: W.H. Freeman.

[19]Massachusetts General Hospital. *Mindfulness meditation training changes brain structure in eight weeks*, *ScienceDaily*, 21 Jan. 2011. Web. 1 Jan. 2013,

[20] Cohen, P. 2001. *Mental Gymnastics Increase Bicep Strength*, New Scientist, 21 Nov. 2012.

[21] Cromie, W., 2002. *Meditation Changes Temperatures: Mind Controls Body in Extreme Experiments*, Harvard University Gazette. 18 April, 2002.

[22] Newberg, A., Waldman, M. 2006. *Born To Believe*, NY: Free Press.

[23] Newberg, A., Waldman, M., 2009. *How God Changes Your Brain*, NY: Ballantine Books.